Social Protection in East Africa

HARNESSING THE FUTURE

This work is published under the responsibility of the Secretary-General of the OECD. The opinions expressed and arguments employed herein do not necessarily reflect the official views of the member countries of the OECD or its Development Centre.

This document and any map included herein are without prejudice to the status of or sovereignty over any territory, to the delimitation of international frontiers and boundaries and to the name of any territory, city or area.

Please cite this publication as:
OECD (2017), *Social Protection in East Africa: Harnessing the Future*, OECD Publishing, Paris.
http://dx.doi.org/10.1787/9789264274228-en

ISBN 978-92-64-27421-1 (print)
ISBN 978-92-64-27422-8 (PDF)

The statistical data for Israel are supplied by and under the responsibility of the relevant Israeli authorities. The use of such data by the OECD is without prejudice to the status of the Golan Heights, East Jerusalem and Israeli settlements in the West Bank under the terms of international law.

Photo credits: Cover © design by the OECD Development Centre

Corrigenda to OECD publications may be found on line at: *www.oecd.org/about/publishing/corrigenda.htm*.

Foreword

The African Union's Agenda 2063 framework reaffirms the centrality of social protection in Africa's strategy for eradicating poverty and ensuring sustainable and equitable development. Yet a number of emerging demographic, economic and environmental trends jeopardise human well-being and challenge Africa's vision for social protection. The genesis of this report lies in the growing realisation that the considerable livelihood threats which lie ahead are unique opportunities for policy makers to shape the future of social protection in the continent in a way that will also foster Africa's broader development.

This study identifies possible futures and explores new paths for action in six countries in East Africa – Ethiopia, Kenya, Mozambique, Tanzania, Uganda and Zambia. It highlights seven grand challenges that confront social protection policy makers in the region and discusses which policy directions are most appropriate for tackling today's social protection needs and preparing for those of tomorrow. A number of these challenges, such as rapid population growth and urbanisation, persistent informality, low domestic resource mobilisation and climate change, are common to sub-Saharan Africa as a whole; the methodology and approach used here will be applicable to many other countries across the region.

This work contributes to the work of the Development Centre on inclusive societies and its objective to help partner countries identify emerging issues, to find innovative solutions to social challenges and build more cohesive societies. This work was undertaken as part of the EU Social Protection Systems Programme, co-funded by the European Union and implemented by the Development Centre and the Government of Finland to support developing countries in building sustainable and inclusive social protection systems.

We hope this exploration will offer new ideas for ways in which all segments of society in the six countries of East Africa covered in the report could work together to promote a long-term perspective on social protection development in the region and, as such, help countries realise their shared vision as spelled out in Agenda 2063.

Mario Pezzini

Director, OECD Development Centre,
and Special Advisor to the OECD Secretary-General on Development

Acknowledgements

Social Protection in East Africa: Harnessing the Future was prepared by the Social Cohesion Unit of the OECD Development Centre as part of the European Union Social Protection Systems Programme.

The team was led by Alexandre Kolev, Head of the Social Cohesion Unit, under the guidance of Mario Pezzini, Director of the OECD Development Centre (DEV) and Special Advisor to the OECD Secretary-General on Development. The report was drafted by Alexandre Kolev and Alexander Pick, drawing from a background paper prepared by Charles Simkins. Justina La provided research assistance.

The report was reviewed by OECD colleagues Alessandro Goglio (Directorate for Employment, Labour and Social Affairs), Juan de Laiglesia (DEV) and Bakary Traoré (DEV). It also benefited from valuable inputs and comments from Alexa DuPlessis (European Union Delegation, Tanzania), Riku Elovainio (DEV), Alessandra Heinemann (DEV), Juergen Hohmann (European Commission), Andrew Mold (United Nations Economic Commission for Africa), Caroline Tassot (DEV) and Timo Voipio (Finnish Institute of Health and Welfare).

The OECD Development Centre's publication team, led by Delphine Grandrieux, turned the draft into a publication. The cover was designed by Aida Buendía.

The European Union Social Protection Systems Programme is co-financed by the European Union, the OECD and the government of Finland.

*This publication has been produced with the assistance of the European Union and Finland. The contents of this publication are the sole responsibility of the OECD and can in no way be taken to reflect the views of the European Union or the government of Finland.

Table of contents

Figures

Tables

Acronyms and abbreviations

ADB	Asian Development Bank
AEO	African Economic Outlook
AfDB	African Development Bank
AIDS	Acquired immunodeficiency syndrome
ART	Antiretroviral therapy
ASPIRE	The Atlas of Social Protection: Indicators of Resilience and Equity
BEPS	Base erosion and profit shifting
CD4	Cluster of differentiation 4
CIT	Corporate income tax
ECD	Early childhood development
EPWP	Expanded Public Works Programme
FAO	Food and Agriculture Organization of the United Nations
FDI	Foreign direct investment
G20	Group of Twenty
GDP	Gross domestic product
GNI	Gross national income
GNP	Gross national product
HIV	Human immunodeficiency virus
HPAEs	High-performing Asian economies
HSNP	Hunger Safety Net Programme
IFAD	International Fund for Agricultural Development
IFPRI	International Food Policy Research Institute
ILO	International Labour Organization
IMF	International Monetary Fund
KSR	Kenyan single registry
LDC	Least developed country
MDC	Matching defined contribution
MDGs	Millennium Development Goals
MGNREGS	Mahatma Ghandi National Rural Employment Guarantee Scheme
NDC	Notional defined contribution
NEETS	Not in education, employment, or training
NGO	Non-governmental organization
NHI	National health insurance
NIMES	National Integrated Monitoring and Evaluation System

NSSF	National Social Security Fund, Kenya
ODA	Official development assistance
ODI	Overseas Development Institute
OECD	Organisation for Economic Co-operation and Development
PAYG	Pay-as-you-go
PIT	Personal income tax
PMT	Proxy means test
PPP	Purchasing power parity
PSNP	Productive Safety Net Programme, Ethiopia
PWP	Public Works Programme
R&D	Research and development
RBA	Retirement Benefits Authority, Kenya
SDGs	Sustainable Development Goals
SHI	Social health insurance
SRH	Sexual and reproductive health
SSA	Sub-Saharan Africa
TASAF	Tanzania Social Action Fund
TFR	Total fertility rate
UBI	Universal basic income
UN DESA	United Nations Department of Economic and Social Affairs
UNCTAD	United Nations Conference on Trade and Development
UNDP	United Nations Development Programme
UNECA	United Nations Economic Commission for Africa
UNESCO	United Nations Educational, Scientific and Cultural Organization
UN-Habitat	United Nations Human Settlements Programme
UNICEF	United Nations Children's Fund
UNRISD	United Nations Research Institute for Social Development
USD	United States dollar
VAT	Value-added tax
WFP	World Food Programme
WHO	World Health Organization
WIDER	World Institute for Development Economics Research
WPP	World Population Projections

Social protection, broadly defined as a set of public instruments to protect people from an absence or substantial reduction in income, lies at the heart of Africa's development strategy. In the African Union's Agenda 2063 framework document, "The Africa We Want", social protection is recognised as both an economic and a social necessity, capable of promoting inclusive, people-driven and sustainable economic growth, eradicating poverty, reducing inequality and generating resilience to future shocks.

The centrality of social protection in Africa's development agenda is reflected by a rapid proliferation of social protection programmes across the continent since the global financial crisis. Social protection is also integral to a number of the Sustainable Development Goals (SDGs), including SDG #1 – To end poverty in all its forms everywhere.

Yet if social protection in Africa is to fulfil its long-term potential as a tool of poverty eradication, resilience and economic development, it not only needs to scale up but also to adapt to the challenges it faces today and to prepare for those of tomorrow. Identifying possible futures and exploring new paths for action is an essential part of this process. This study provides a long-term perspective on the future of social protection in six countries in East Africa: Ethiopia, Kenya, Mozambique, Tanzania, Uganda and Zambia.

According to the most recent population projections by the United Nations, the population of sub-Saharan Africa will quadruple over the course of the 21st century, increasing from 1 billion in 2016 to almost 4 billion in 2100. How the region manages this population growth will be central to its long-term prospects. If fertility rates decline significantly, dependency ratios across the region will follow suit, offering the potential of a large demographic dividend provided that working-age individuals are productively employed. However, if fertility rates do not decline and if the rapidly-expanding ranks of the working age population cannot find productive work, intense political, economic, social and environmental pressures will arise. The age structure of the population in the six countries will be dominated by a youth bulge for the next 20 or 30 years. However, the proportion of elderly individuals will start to rise rapidly thereafter.

Africa's population boom will be accompanied by rapid urbanisation, a phenomenon which has the capacity to promote economic development but which will also require large-scale improvements to urban infrastructure and services. Urbanisation will also change the dynamics of poverty across the six countries from a predominantly rural problem. Nonetheless, urbanisation in East Africa is starting from a very low base: the rural population in a number of countries will still be larger than the urban population in 2050. These individuals will be at ever-increasing risk from the effects of climate change, which will affect the region dramatically and in different ways.

While Africa's long-term economic prospects are positive, GDP growth alone cannot mitigate the challenges that the region confronts. Although the economies of the six countries have grown rapidly since 2000, population growth has dampened the impact of this growth on per capita incomes. While it is unlikely that recent growth rates will be sustained far into the future, the model presented in this study shows how the growth in the working-age population relative to the number of dependants could support the economies in all six countries, outweighing the impact of continued population growth.

Ensuring new entrants to the labour market are productively employed will be a priority if a demographic dividend is to materialise. An average of 7 million new jobs will be required per year across the six countries if current levels of employment are to be maintained. In the absence of faster structural change, the majority of these jobs will be in agriculture and other informal activities, and agriculture will remain a major component of economic output even in 2065.

The rate of poverty reduction will depend on the interaction between GDP growth, population growth and the level of inequality. According to projections presented in this report, the first Sustainable Development Goal – to eradicate poverty everywhere – will not be achieved in any of the sample countries for a long time after 2030. On a 50-year view, only three of the countries will have poverty headcount ratios of less than 5% against the USD 1.90 benchmark. In absolute terms, the number of individuals in extreme poverty will decline only slightly across the region between now and 2065.

The projections detailed in this report indicate seven major challenges confronting social protection policy makers in East Africa:

1. **Solving the last mile problem to reach the poorest of the poor.** The poverty rate has fallen across Africa in the past 25 years but it is proving difficult to reach the extreme poor. Spending on social assistance will need to increase substantially to reach these groups and targeting policies will need to prioritise minimising errors of exclusion over preventing leakage to the non-poor.

2. **Promoting social insurance in a context of high informality.** Coverage of social insurance across Africa is very low, reflecting the fact that only workers in formal employment usually have access to such arrangements. Social insurance arrangements must adapt to the fact that the majority of the workforce will remain in the informal sector 50 years from now.

3. **Confronting the employment challenge.** Social protection interventions need to address the needs of the working-age population. In East Africa, public works programmes are emerging as an important response to the challenge of providing work but need to operate at a larger scale without doing harm to the broader labour market.

4. **Harnessing a demographic dividend.** For the countries of East Africa to harness a demographic dividend, they will need to ensure fertility rates continue to fall and accelerate improvements in human and physical capital in order to enhance the future productivity of the economy.

5. **Taking social protection to the cities.** As East Africa's urban populations grow, so too will the proportion of poor individuals living in cities, and slums in particular. Social assistance programmes, which until now have focused on rural areas, need to adapt to towns and cities.

6. **Adapting to climate change.** Scalable social protection programmes promote resilience to climate change, allowing individuals not only to respond quickly to climate-related shocks but also to diversify their livelihoods and "climate-proof" their land and homes in preparation for such a shock.

7. **Increasing financing for social protection.** A significant increase in the resources available for social protection is required if the sector is to meet the challenges identified in this report. Raising these revenues on a sustainable basis will require considerable effort and careful consideration of who bears the burden of domestic taxation.

Addressing these challenges will require a systemic approach that promotes coherence between programmes, policies and institutions and which integrates social protection with other sectoral strategies. The challenges will also require greater capacity to design, deliver and monitor social protection programmes, as well as clear communication between governments and social partners, including organised labour, civil society and business. Although these are long-term challenges, the policy response should start today.

The 21st century has been a period of great achievement for most countries in Africa. Sustained and robust economic growth and greater political stability across the region have accompanied a significant decline in poverty and major improvements in living standards. According to the World Bank, the proportion of people living in extreme poverty fell from 57% in 1990 to 43% in 2012, while the rate of mortality among children under 5 has almost halved, from 173 per 1 000 live births in 1995 to 92 in 2013. Net primary school enrolment rose from 59% in 1999 to 79% in 2012.

Nonetheless, there remains a long way to go: of the world's 48 least developed countries (as defined by the United Nations), 34 are located in sub-Saharan Africa. Despite the decline in headcount poverty, the absolute number of poor individuals increased by 100 million between 1995 and 2012 as a result of population growth. Moreover, the gains achieved in the past 15 years are fragile: significant numbers of those who have emerged from poverty are at great risk of falling back.

Social protection is an effective means of sustaining the decline in poverty and protecting those individuals who have emerged from poverty from falling back. Moreover, there is an increasing body of evidence demonstrating the capacity of social protection programmes to promote human development. A rapid expansion of social protection in Africa since the global financial crisis reflects the important and multiple benefits social protection can generate at both the micro and the macro level. Today, nearly every country in the continent implements a social safety net and the number of countries implementing a cash transfer programme more than doubled between 2010 and 2014.

However, many more people are excluded from social protection in Africa than are covered by these arrangements. Only 11% of the poorest 20% of households are covered by social assistance in sub-Saharan Africa, compared with 21% in South Asia, 50% in Eastern Europe and Central Asia and 58% in Latin America. Coverage of other social protection instruments – social welfare services, social insurance and labour market policies – is lower still. In the case of social insurance, less than 10% of the population is covered across the region, meaning that an overwhelming majority of today's workforce population has little or no income protection either now or in preparation for their old age.

The African Union's Agenda 2063 framework, "The Africa We Want", recognises the potential of social protection and places it at the heart of the continent's development strategy. Building on the Social Protection Framework adopted by the African Union in 2008, Agenda 2063 establishes two ambitious targets for social protection systems across the continent: i) to raise spending on social protection to 5% of GDP (from an average of 2% currently) in order to establish social protection floors so that no citizen is without access to a basic income or essential health care; and ii) to extend coverage of contributory social security arrangements into the informal and rural sector in order to protect household incomes.

Thanks in part to the international development community, greater resources are being made available for social protection in Africa. Countries across the continent are developing long-term strategies for expanding provision, which in turn are reflected through their national development plans. At the same time, social protection programmes are evolving and innovating to better respond to national needs and priorities, supported by an important increase in the level of co-operation between countries in the Global South in addressing social protection challenges.

Yet even as governments look to scale up social protection to deal with the challenges of today, a number of demographic, economic and environmental trends are emerging that could either strengthen or jeopardise Africa's development and its vision for social protection. The region's population boom could result in a significant demographic dividend provided that fertility rates fall and the fast-growing workforce is productively employed; if these not conditions are attained, population growth will impose a major brake on development. Rapid urbanisation has the potential to transform societies but, if it is not properly managed, can instead constrain progress in improving living conditions and eliminating extreme poverty.

At the same time, robust growth in many African economies since the early 2000s has not been accompanied by major changes to the structure of economic activity or employment, with the result that manufacturing has barely grown across the continent and agriculture remains a dominant source of income and livelihoods. This continued reliance on low-productivity agricultural activities not only limits Africa's potential to increase incomes and generate new jobs but it also leaves populations and economies at risk from climate change – a phenomenon to which Africa is especially vulnerable.

In the six countries which form the basis for this study – Ethiopia, Kenya, Mozambique, Tanzania, Uganda and Zambia – social protection is well established on the political agenda and scaling-up significantly but confronts many of the challenges facing Africa as a whole. These countries exhibit sufficient similarities to represent East Africa in comparison with other regions but are also different enough to allow comparison between them so as to better understand the dynamics around demographics, structural change, poverty and inequality.

The study looks forward over the next 50 years to explore what might be the main drivers of demand for social protection and identify appropriate policy responses. The report is structured as follows. Chapter 1 analyses major demographic and environmental challenges facing the six sample countries over the next 50 years, including the impact of the current population boom on the age structure of the population, urbanisation, changing health needs and cross-border migration. Chapter 2 identifies future socio-economic trends in the six countries based on an economic model which provides long-term projections for income growth, poverty levels, and the structure of the labour market and economic output up to 2065. The final chapter highlights seven grand challenges that confront social protection planners and proposes potential policy responses.

Confronting massive demographic and environmental challenges

According to projections published by the United Nations in 2015, the population of sub-Saharan Africa will quadruple over the course of the 21st century, increasing from 1 billion in 2016 to fractionally below 4 billion in 2100. Thanks to rapid growth in the size of the working-age population, there will be substantial declines in dependency ratios across the continent, offering the potential of a large demographic dividend if current levels of employment and productivity are maintained or improve. However, high rates of population growth dilute economy-wide income gains and place considerable strain on basic services – an area where governments in the region are already under pressure to deliver.

The demographics of East Africa are currently characterised by high fertility rates, low life expectancies, high population growth rates, young populations and high dependency ratios. Rapid population growth is projected for all the sample countries but it will be fastest in Zambia and slowest in Ethiopia. The age structure of the population will change significantly across the countries: every age group will grow in absolute terms but in relative terms the size of the infant and school-aged cohorts has peaked while the youth cohort is growing in both relative and absolute terms, placing pressure on the education system and the labour market. The working age population will grow strongly – both relatively and especially in absolute terms – over the next 50 years. The elderly population will grow slowly at first before expanding faster than any other cohort in relative terms as today's youth bulge reaches retirement age.

These projections are not set in stone. Governments in the six countries have published policies to reduce fertility rates but there are worrying signs that the fertility decline across the sample is stalling, a phenomenon that requires an urgent response. The determinants of fertility are complex and difficult to control directly through public policy. Increases or improvements in income, health, women's education, female labour force participation and urbanisation can all play a key role in reducing fertility; so too can social and cultural factors.

With the changes in the age structure of the population, it is expected that a higher proportion of the population will suffer from chronic conditions in the future while the burden of communicable diseases will decline. There have been major successes in controlling communicable diseases but HIV/AIDS and malaria will remain a drain on public health services and emerging diseases can wipe out gains achieved in terms of health outcomes.

Sub-Saharan Africa's population boom will be accompanied by large-scale urbanisation. According to UN projections, Africa is expected to be 56% urban in 2050, versus 40% in 2014. East Africa is the least urbanised region in the world today but a long-term average annual urban population growth of 4% is projected across the sample countries. Nonetheless, the rural population in a number of the sample countries will still be larger than the urban population in 2050. Population growth will be concentrated at the interface of urban and rural areas; urbanisation will be driven primarily by building new cities rather than expanding existing ones.

According to the UN Population Projections, international migration will be not a major determinant of population change in the sample countries: there will be net emigration of just under 5 million people from the six countries in the next 50 years, and just under 8.5 million from East Africa as a whole. This appears very conservative given the unprecedented level of population growth across the sample countries (especially among working age cohorts), the sharp increase in population densities and the potential impact of climate change. Population growth might be a push factor for emigration, with a high bound estimate of the surplus of labour or potential supply of migrants from the region standing at 140 million. At the same time, population ageing in wealthier countries will be a pull factor. However, labour flows are highly regulated and there is not an obvious destination for East African emigrants.

Climate change will affect East Africa dramatically and in different ways. Current models indicate that climate change will affect both temperatures and rainfall levels. The impact of climate change will not only be felt inland; rising sea levels and associated coastal erosion will also be a major concern for residents in coastal areas. At the same time, climate change will be associated with numerous health risks which the poorest individuals are least able to bear. The region's capacity to feed itself and meet its needs in terms of water provision will be further strained. By and large, the rural poor will be disproportionately affected by climate change due to their heavily reliance on agriculture.

Forecasting economic and social trends for long-term social protection planning

Economic growth rates across Africa have improved markedly since their stagnation in the 1980s and 1990s. However, population growth has dampened the impact of economic growth on per capita incomes. While East Africa is currently outperforming the rest of Africa, it is unlikely that the growth rates experienced in recent years will be sustained far into the future. Projections in this paper indicate that favourable demographics could support robust growth in all six countries over the long term but there are significant upside and downside risks to this projection: increased productivity as a result of accelerated structural change would yield higher growth rates, while an increase in unemployment would likely have the opposite effect.

If the process of structural change continues at its current slow pace across the six countries, agriculture will remain a major component of economic output even in 2065, and the majority of the workforce will still be employed either in agriculture or other informal activities. A total of 7 million new jobs will be required every year across the sample countries to absorb new entrants to the labour market if current levels of labour force participation are to be maintained. The absorptive capacity of agriculture will be critical to clearing the labour market but the effects of climate change pose a major threat to productivity in the sector as well as to rural livelihoods more generally.

The rate of future poverty declines will depend not only on the rate of income per capita growth but also how incomes gains are distributed across the economy. At present, poverty rates and the level of inequality vary significantly across the six countries. Over the long term, poverty is projected to fall furthest in Ethiopia and remain highest in Zambia. Based on these projections, the first Sustainable Development Goal – to eradicate poverty everywhere – will not be achieved in any of the sample countries for a long time after 2030: on a 50-year view, only three will have poverty rates below 5% against the USD 1.90 benchmark of extreme poverty. In absolute terms, the number of poor individuals will decline very little across the region between now and 2065 due to the rate of population growth.

Towards a long-term perspective on social protection in East Africa

This report identifies seven major challenges that social protection policy makers will confront over the long term: i) the last mile problem of eradicating extreme poverty; ii) promoting social insurance in a context of high informality; iii) confronting the employment challenge; iv) harnessing a demographic dividend; v) rapid urbanisation; vi) climate change; and vii) financing a step-change in social protection spending.

These are long-term challenges that need a policy response in the short term. The challenges are also inter-related, which will require a systematic approach that ensures coherence across the social protection sector at a policy, administrative and institutional level and which connects social protection to other government initiatives in sectors such as labour, the environment, agriculture and economic development. A capacity-development strategy will also be required for implementing some or all of the policies proposed here, while the participation of social partners in meeting these challenges will be essential both for securing popular support and for successful implementation.

Solving the "last mile" problem of eradicating extreme poverty. Data suggests the six countries are spending enough on social assistance to eliminate extreme poverty. However, this expenditure is not reaching the poorest households and there is significant leakage to the non-poor. Pursuing perfect targeting of transfers is likely to be a losing battle; higher spending and an emphasis on reducing exclusion errors (at a cost of tolerating inclusion errors) is the most viable means of reaching those most in need in the short term and will yield long-term benefits in terms of reducing poverty and inequality.

Enhancing social insurance coverage in a context of high informality. Coverage of social insurance across the sample countries is very low because these arrangements are typically accessible only to the formally employed. Governments need to adapt social insurance to a context where the majority of the workforce will remain in agricultural and informal employment 50 years from now. Failing to do so will leave large parts of the population vulnerable to falling into poverty in the event of an income shock or when they can no longer work.

Confronting the employment challenge. Public works programmes are already emerging across East Africa as an important part of the policy response to the rapid growth in the working age population. These programmes are capable of making an important contribution both at an individual level and for wider communities, but to do so they must meet a number of important conditions in terms of generating useful work and providing participants with skills they can use in the labour market.

Harnessing a demographic dividend. To harness a demographic dividend, it will be necessary to accelerate the decline in fertility rates and to promote productivity through enhancements to human and physical capital. Social protection can contribute to a decline in fertility by promoting women's access to health, education and the labour market, while enhancing pension provision can achieve a similar impact by reducing the elderly's reliance on their children for support in old age. Social protection enhances productivity by promoting gains in human capital (in particular through early childhood development initiatives) and higher saving rates.

Adapting social protection to rapid urbanisation. As urban populations continue their rapid growth in East Africa, so too will demand for social protection arrangements that are tailored to urban settings. Extending social protection to urban areas will require a much better understanding of the needs of city-dwellers, especially those living in slums.

Resilience to climate change. Climate change poses a massive, unpredictable and escalating threat to livelihoods in East Africa. Social protection programmes are able not only to help individuals withstand a climate-related shock but can also help households and communities adapt to climate change and mitigate its effects.

Increasing financing for social protection without hurting the poor. For social protection to achieve its potential, the African Union calculates that annual spending should more than double across the region to 5% of GDP. Significant domestic resource mobilisation will be required; care should be taken to protect the poor from shouldering too much of this burden.

Key recommendations

System level

Establish an integrated framework for social assistance, social insurance and labour market policies

- Identify the linkages between different instruments to ensure coverage across the life cycle.
- Connect the programmes, budgets and institutions operating across the social protection sector to facilitate co-ordination and develop integrated systems, financing plans and strategies.
- Leverage the economic multiplier effects achievable through social protection by integrating it within broader development plans and in strategies for achieving the Sustainable Development Goals and the objectives of Agenda 2063.

Ensure that social protection is adequately financed while reconciling the objectives of tax and social policies

- Prioritise increases in direct taxes when developing strategies for domestic resource mobilisation; efforts to improve compliance will need to focus not only on domestic taxpayers but should also target multinational companies.
- Assess the incidence of taxes and transfers and their combined impact on poverty and inequality to ensure that the fiscal system works for the poor.
- Eliminate or reduce subsidies for food and fuel to free up resources for social protection schemes.

- Control spending on civil service pensions by establishing transparent and sustainable financing mechanisms.

Use social protection to promote individual and economy-wide productivity gains

- Increase investment in early childhood development to promote cognitive development and skills acquisition among tomorrow's workforce.
- Use training schemes to promote individual productivity and entrepreneurial skills.
- Leverage the potential of social protection instruments to promote investment in physical capital.

Maximise the potential of social protection for women's empowerment

- Promote women's access to health, education, family-planning services and the labour market through social protection.
- Ensure social protection is gender-sensitive and does not impose additional constraints on female participants, either in terms of time use or by reinforcing harmful social norms.
- Promote gender parity in social insurance arrangements through mechanisms that compensate women for the time they spend out of the labour market caring for children or other family members.

Adjust social protection strategies to address the needs of a growing urban population

- Devise implementation modalities to overcome challenges associated with the urban setting in terms of targeting social assistance.
- Work with local government to integrate social protection into urban development strategies.
- Consider the use of public works programmes as a means of supporting the provision of essential services in a context of rapid urbanisation.

Place social protection at the fore of climate-change adaptation strategies

- Develop scalable social protection programmes which can respond to climate-induced shocks quicker, more accurately and at lower cost than humanitarian assistance.
- Link social protection programmes to early warning systems to provide support for vulnerable groups before a climate-related shock occurs.
- Promote micro-insurance for farmers to mitigate the unpredictable and varied threat to livelihoods posed by climate change.

Progressively enhance the statistical basis for social protection policy making at four levels

- Enhance civil registration and census collection to understand population characteristics and dynamics.
- Carry out regular household surveys with social protection modules to ascertain the needs of the population, target interventions and assess the impact of social protection.
- Establish single registries and Management Information Systems that are unified across the social protection sector to identify beneficiaries and link them to appropriate interventions.
- Build rigorous monitoring and evaluation mechanisms for individual social protection programmes to understand their impact and inform their design.

Programme level

Place social assistance at the forefront of poverty-reduction strategies

- Increase social assistance spending to better reach the extreme poor and reduce inequality.
- Adapt social assistance to evolving social and demographic trends, including the dynamic nature of poverty, the changing age structure of the population and rapid urbanisation.
- Prioritise a reduction in errors of exclusion in the short term and improvements in administrative capacity to reduce inclusion errors over the longer term.

Expand innovative and flexible social insurance arrangements to protect the growing informal workforce

- Explore the introduction of subsidised or matching contributions from the government to incentivise participation in social insurance arrangements.
- Establish an enabling environment in financial and capital markets to ensure that contributions to funded arrangements generate returns and are protected against investment risks.
- Leverage labour associations, cooperatives and formal enterprises that employ large numbers of informal workers in order to promote contributions from informal sector workers.

Invest in public works programmes to accommodate rapid growth in the working-age population

- Scale up public works programmes and ensure that these interventions are accessible to the large youth cohorts who will enter the labour market in the next 50 years.
- Align public works programmes to broader national development strategies while involving local government and communities in identification and implementation of projects.
- Expand public works programmes beyond a focus on infrastructure towards environmental and social services.

Chapter 1

Confronting massive demographic and environmental challenges

This chapter examines the demographic and environmental challenges that lie ahead in six East African states as the first step in identifying key parameters that will shape the future of social protection in the region. The six countries – Ethiopia, Kenya, Mozambique, Tanzania, Uganda and Zambia – exhibit similar demographic trends. However, differences exist between them that will have important implications not only for their population in the future but also for their broader development.

The world's last and largest population boom

According to population projections published by the United Nations in 2015, the population of sub-Saharan Africa is projected to increase from 1 billion in 2016 to 2 billion in 2046 and reach fractionally below 4 billion in 2100 (UN DESA, 2015a). By 2100, sub-Saharan Africa will account for 35% of the world's total population, up from 13% in 2016 (Figure 1.1).

Figure 1.1. **Global population size by region, 1950-2100**

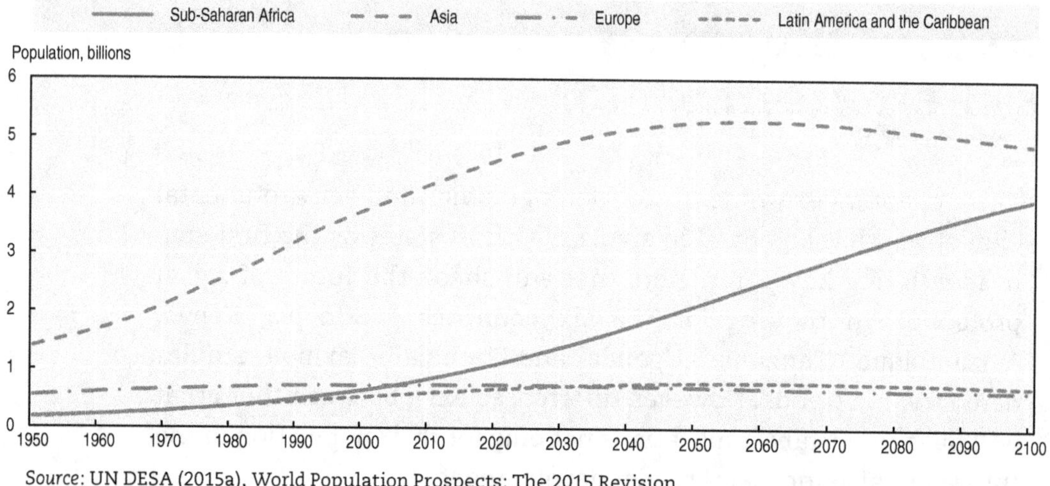

Source: UN DESA (2015a), World Population Prospects: The 2015 Revision.

In 2010-15, East Africa's annual population growth rate was 2.8%, more than double the 1.2% growth rate for the world as a whole. Due to a combination of high fertility rates and significant increases in life expectancies across the six countries, rapid population growth is projected to continue between 2015 and 2065 for all the sample countries. The populations of Zambia, Uganda, Tanzania and Mozambique will more than treble in size, while Ethiopia's population will register the slowest growth but will still double over this timeframe (Figure 1.2). These growth rates will have a bearing on the rate at which governments in the region can meet demand for improved basic services and the provision of public infrastructure (Foster and Briceño-Garmendia, 2010).

Figure 1.2. **Population size of the six sample countries, 2015 and 2065**

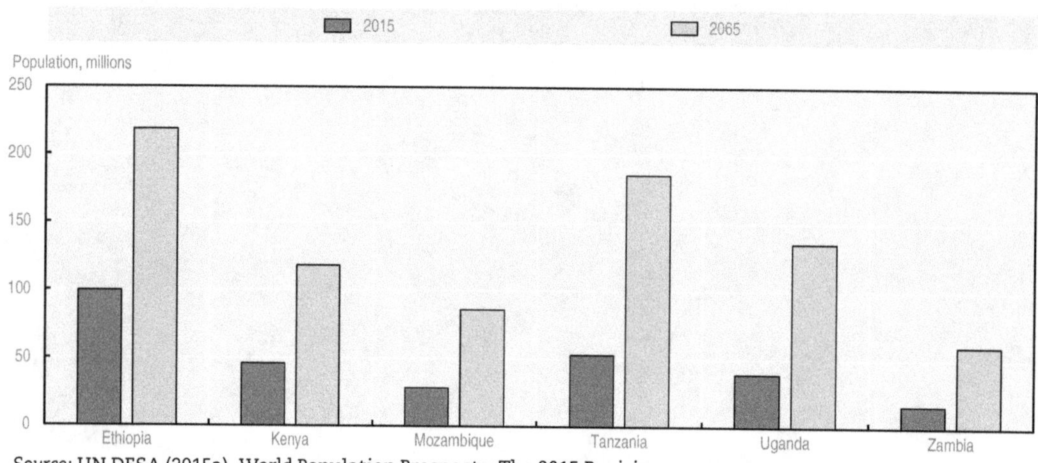

Source: UN DESA (2015a), World Population Prospects: The 2015 Revision.

Figure 1.3. **Fertility rates across sample countries, 1965-2065**

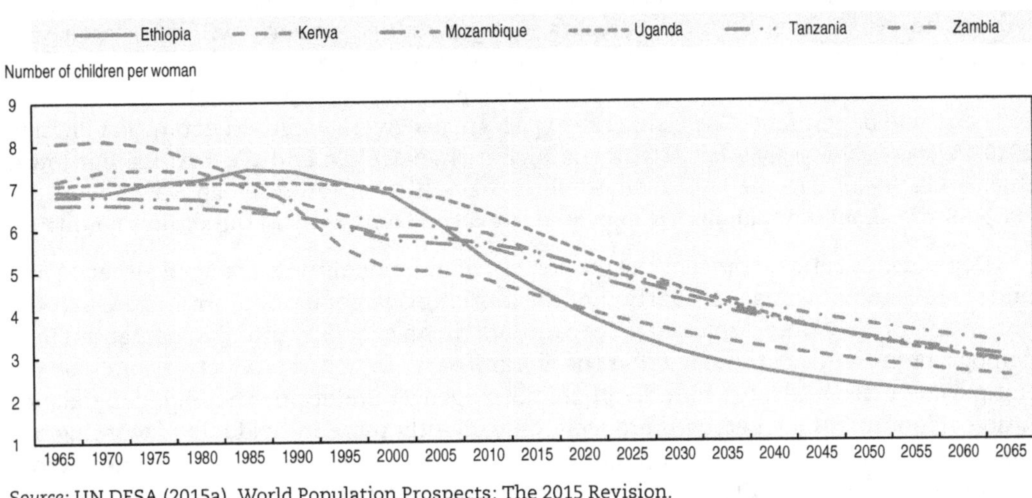

Source: UN DESA (2015a), World Population Prospects: The 2015 Revision.

The sample countries are at an early or mid-stage in the fertility transition (Muhoza, Broekhuis and Hooimeijer, 2014).[1] As shown by Figure 1.3, their fertility rates have declined significantly since the 1970s (though at different rates in different countries). However, there is evidence that the decline might be stalling. Goujon, Lutz and KC (2015) identify Kenya, Mozambique, Tanzania and Zambia as countries where the fertility decline has stalled, while Bongaarts (2008) concludes the same about Ethiopia and Uganda (using a slightly different methodology). The cause of this stalling is the subject of considerable speculation but cannot be identified with much certainty given the numerous determinants of fertility and the fact that fertility rates differ significantly within the same country depending on income level, education and place of residence. The variation in fertility across and within the six countries can be attributed in significant part to the complex impact of HIV/AIDS in shaping individuals' reproductive choices (Ezeh, Mberu and Emina, 2009).

Figure 1.4. **Aggregate population pyramids for the six sample countries, 2015, 2040 and 2065**

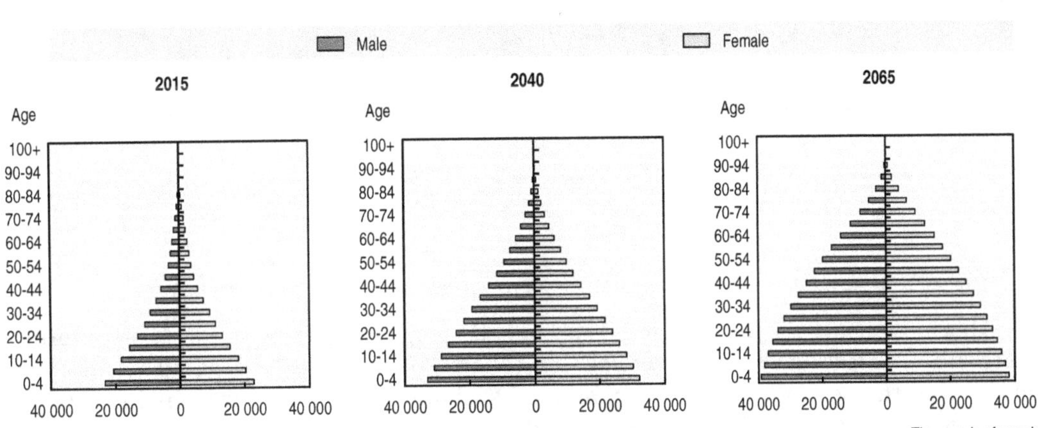

Source: Authors' calculations based on UN DESA (2015a), World Population Prospects: The 2015 Revision.

The age structure of the populations will change dramatically. In 2015, children aged 0-14 made up 44.6% of the population across the sample countries; by 2065, this figure will fall to 29.2%. Over the next 50 years, today's younger cohorts will work their way up the age pyramid (Figure 1.4), shifting the bulge from youth (15-24 years) to working age and then to old age. Rapid growth in the elderly population will start no later than 2035 and will be reinforced by rising life expectancies. Average life expectancy at birth in 2010-15 was 60.5 in East Africa, which is higher than Middle and West Africa but lower than other regions in the world, all of which have life expectancies above 70 years. By 2060-65, life expectancy at birth is expected to exceed 70 years in all the sample countries.

Dependency ratios represent the proportion of individuals who are aged either 14 and under or 65 and older as a proportion of the working age population. An increase in the proportion of "producers" relative to "consumers" in an economy offers the potential for a demographic dividend, provided that the workforce is employed productively. Across the sample countries, the large number of children aged 14 underpins the high dependency ratio evident in 2015, whereby there were only slightly more individuals of working age than dependants in the entire population. If the decline in fertility rates resumes across the six countries, this will reduce the size of the child population relative to the working age population and will produce a significant decline in the dependency ratio between 2015 and 2065 (Figure 1.5), though this decline will decelerate as today's youth cohort reaches retirement age. The dependency ratio will fall fastest and furthest in Ethiopia and slowest and least far in Zambia; Ethiopia's dependency ratio is projected to start rising from around 2055 onwards due to growth in the elderly population.

Figure 1.5. **Dependency ratios in the sample countries, 1965 to 2065**

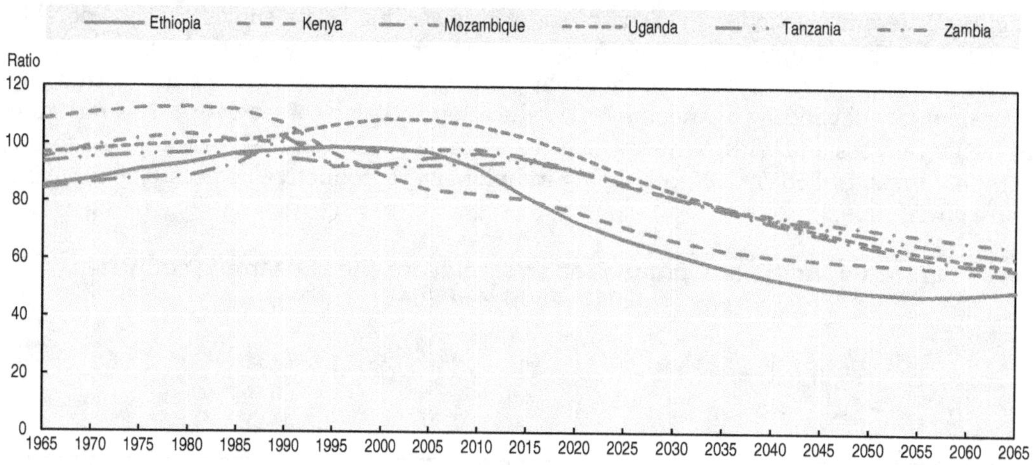

Source: UN DESA (2015a), World Population Prospects: The 2015 Revision.

Today's youth will be the largest cohort ever to enter the labour force

All age groups grow in absolute terms over the projection period but in relative terms there will be important variations between age cohorts. To illustrate the dynamics of different age cohorts, this section disaggregates the age distribution into four groups: childhood (aged 0-14); youth; (15-24); working age (25-59); and elderly (aged 60 and above). The distinction between the "youth" and the "working-age" cohorts is acknowledged to be artificial due to the high labour force participation rate among young people across the region: Sub-Saharan Africa is the only region in the world where the labour force participation rate of the youth (aged 15-24) did not decline between 2007 and 2014 (ILO, 2015).

Figure 1.6. Children (aged 0-14), as a percentage of total population and absolute number between 2015 and 2065

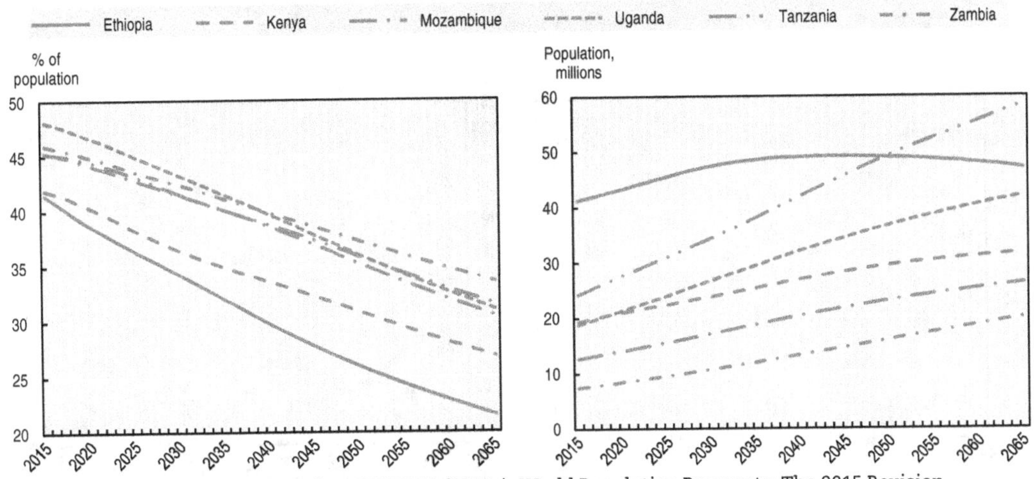

Source: Authors' calculations based on UN DESA (2015a), World Population Prospects: The 2015 Revision.

The size of the infant and school-aged cohorts relative to the population as a whole has peaked but in absolute terms the number will continue to rise. Children aged between 0 and 14 currently comprise between 40% and 50% of the population in all the sample countries. This proportion is projected to decrease throughout the survey period (Figure 1.6) as a result of the decline in fertility rates. However, in absolute terms, the number of children will increase steadily over the projection period (fastest in Tanzania and slowest in Ethiopia), imposing significant and sustained pressure on the region's education systems.

In 2015, the youth cohort (defined as individuals aged 15-24) accounted for around 20% of the total population across the sample (Figure 1.7). This proportion will grow in all countries for the next 10-20 years (with the exception of Ethiopia, where it will peak sooner) before declining slowly over time. With educational enrolment among this group presently low and unemployment high relative to the economy as a whole, it is widely acknowledged that this cohort represents a significant and urgent challenge to policy makers. By 2050, the size of the youth cohort will grow by 123.8%.

Figure 1.7. Youth (ages 15-24), as a percentage of total population and absolute number between 2015 and 2065

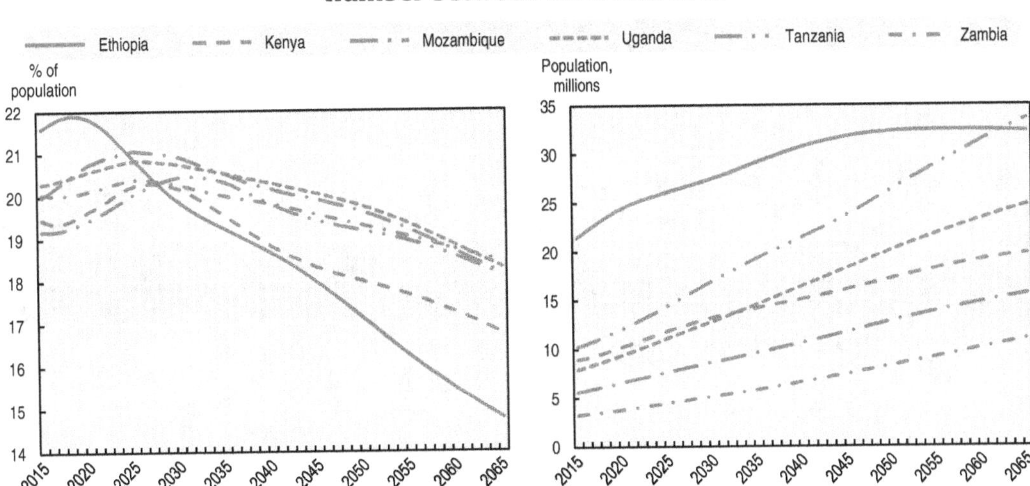

Source: UN DESA (2015a), World Population Prospects: The 2015 Revision.

Figure 1.8. **Working age adults (aged 25-59), in each country between 2015 and 2065 in absolute terms and as a percentage of total population**

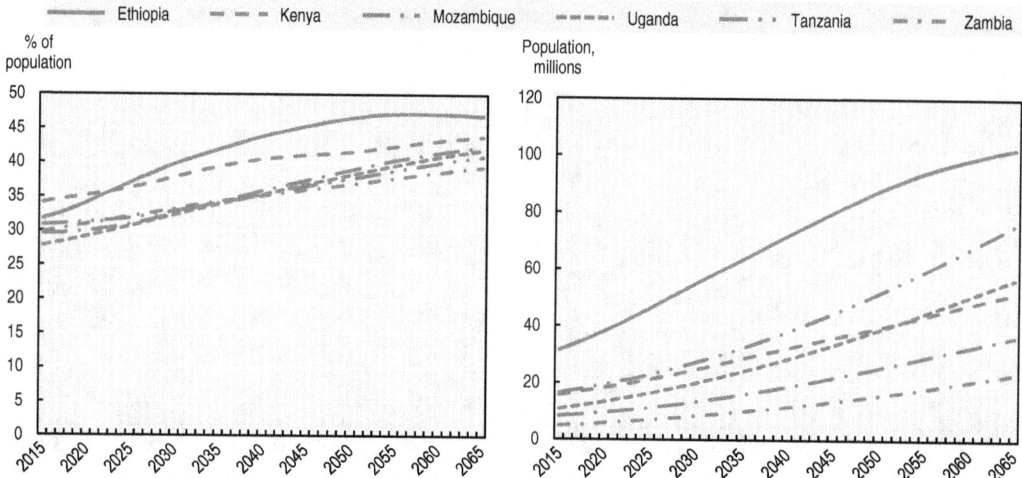

Source: UN DESA (2015a), World Population Prospects: The 2015 Revision.

Figure 1.8 shows the number of working age adults across the six countries. This cohort accounted for around 30% of the population in 2015 across the six countries and will continue to grow strongly until 2065, although this growth levels off towards the end of the timeframe relative to the population as a whole. Ethiopia is the only country where the working-age population will exceed 60% of the population as a whole. The rapid growth in the working age population – both in relative and absolute terms – will drive a significant change in the composition of the global workforce. In 2015, sub-Saharan Africa accounted for 11% of the world's working-age population (age 15-59); in 2065, it will account for 28%.

Figure 1.9. **Adults aged over 60 in each country between 2015 and 2065 in absolute terms and as a percentage of total population**

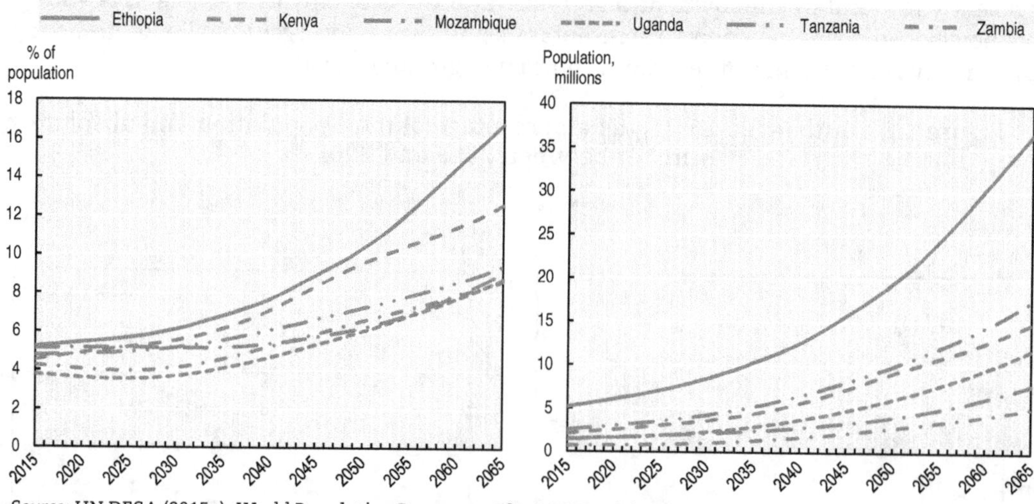

Source: UN DESA (2015a), World Population Prospects: The 2015 Revision.

By 2065, the present youth cohort will have reached retirement age. As Figure 1.9 shows, the proportion of the population aged over 60 grows slowly at first before rising rapidly between 2030 and 2040 – especially so in the case of Ethiopia and Kenya, where the relative size of the elderly population is projected to double between 2030 and 2065. The focus on expanding contributory social protection arrangements today reflects this challenge, distant though it may seem: guaranteeing an adequate retirement income in the future requires that workers set money aside for the majority of their career.

It is worth remembering that, while there is scope for the fertility rate to decline, the ageing of the population is inevitable (barring catastrophe). Indeed, any success the region achieves in reducing the fertility rate faster than was projected by the United Nations in 2015 (Box 1.1) will be tempered by the fact that such a reduction would accelerate the ageing of the population.

Box 1.1. The pace of development is likely to determine future fertility trends

Accelerating the fertility decline is an explicit policy goal across all six countries, each of which has published at least one population policy.[a] Fertility is negatively correlated with a number of key developmental variables such as income growth, female education, female labour force participation, falling mortality (in particular infant mortality) and urbanisation – variables which are often positively correlated with each other.

However, the determinants of reproductive behaviour are not solely economic – social and cultural factors can play a very important role. The complex determinants of fertility are reflected by the significant variation that exists within countries. In Ethiopia, for example, the total fertility rate (TFR) in Addis Ababa is 1.5, compared with 5.5 in rural parts of the country and 7.1 in Somali – one of three regions where the TFR increased between 2005 and 2011 despite the overall decline nationally (Federal Democratic Republic of Ethiopia, 2014).

Figure 1.10. Family planning indicators, 1970-2015

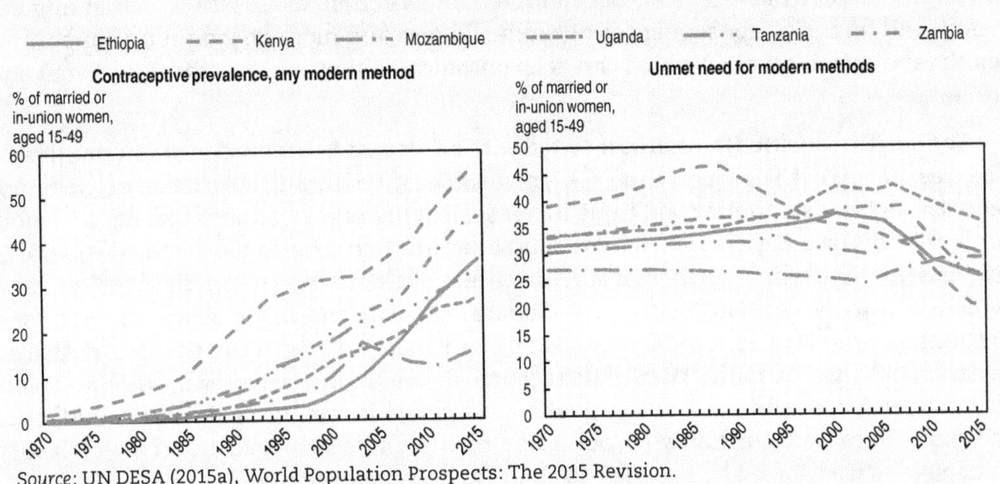

Source: UN DESA (2015a), World Population Prospects: The 2015 Revision.

Many countries have shown that increasing availability and access to family planning services can contribute to lowering the TFR (Cleland, 2006; USAID, 2012). The evidence from East Africa is encouraging. Figure 1.10 (left-hand panel) captures the percentage of women of reproductive age (between 15 to 49 years old) who are currently married or in a civil union and using modern methods of contraception. This indicator has risen sharply across all the sample countries since the early 1990s (earlier in the case of Kenya). There is wide variation between countries, with Kenya having the highest estimated prevalence of modern contraception in 2015 (at 56.0%) and Mozambique the lowest, at 16.0%.

> Box 1.1. **The pace of development is likely to determine future fertility trends** (cont.)
>
> The East African average for all forms of contraception was 40% in 2015, which is low relative to Northern and Southern Africa (53% and 64% respectively) but high relative to Middle and Western Africa (23% and 17% respectively). Unmet need for modern contraception methods (right-hand panel of Figure 1.10) reflects the percentage of married or in-union women of reproductive age who are not using any method of contraception but would like to stop or postpone childbearing. Unmet need is lowest in Kenya and highest in Uganda, while Zambia is the only county where the trend is currently increasing. Eastern, Western and Middle Africa have the highest unmet demand for contraception globally.
>
> *Note:* See Ethiopia (1993), Kenya (1967, 1986, 2012); Mozambique (1999); Zambia (1989, 2007) Tanzania (1992, 2006), Uganda (1995, 2008, 2011).
>
> *Sources:* Cleland (2006), "Family planning: the unfinished agenda"; Federal Democratic Republic of Ethiopia (2014), *Population Stabilization Report;* USAID (2012), *Three Successful Sub-Saharan Africa Family Planning Programs: Lessons for Meeting the MDGs,* USAID/Africa Bureau, USAID/Population and Reproductive Health, Ethiopia Federal Ministry of Health, Malawi Ministry of Health, Rwanda Ministry of Health.

The demographic transition will be accompanied by changing health needs

The demographic transition that will occur in East Africa will be accompanied an epidemiological transition. The combined effect of these two trends is an increase in the size of the older population with an increasing risk of chronic diseases. The epidemiological transition is also linked to changes in behaviour (such as nutritional practices) as well as to environmental factors such as increased exposure to traffic-related air pollution in a context of rapid urbanisation. An increase in chronic conditions affects health policies – the response to health problems becomes less about cure and more about *ex ante* prevention and *ex post* disease management. Social protection will thus focus less on mitigating the (health and financial) consequences of sudden illness and more on long-term support for health (and social) services which can keep chronically ill people healthy, functional and productive.

The health transition is often associated with a decrease in the burden of communicable diseases, though it is argued that the prevalence of communicable diseases does not decrease as fast as chronic conditions increase, leaving many countries facing a "double burden" of disease (Dye, 2014). Across sub-Saharan Africa, there has been considerable progress in controlling communicable diseases: the number of deaths from malaria (which is heavily concentrated in sub-Saharan Africa) has fallen from an estimated 839 000 deaths in 2000 to 438 000 in 2015 and there has also been a clear drop in diarrheal diseases and lower respiratory infections (such as pneumonia). However, communicable diseases remain a burden on public health systems while emerging diseases, epidemics and pandemics can quickly wipe out some of the gains achieved in terms of health outcomes, as was shown by the 2014-16 Ebola crisis in West Africa.

HIV/AIDS remains one of the major health challenges in the sample countries. Annex 1.A2 shows prevalence rates since 2000 and years lost to AIDS disability as a percentage of years lost to disabilities of all kinds. Ethiopia appears to be the least affected, followed by Tanzania, Kenya, Uganda; Mozambique and Zambia have the highest prevalence rates. Reported trends vary too: since 2001, the trend has been downward in Ethiopia, Kenya and Tanzania, up in Uganda, and rising to a plateau in 2009 in Mozambique and Zambia.

Years lost to AIDS disability as a percentage of years lost to all disability in the 15-19 age group is no more than 5% in all six countries. The percentages rise among the 30-59 age group, exceeding 12% in Mozambique and Zambia. Prevalence rates and disabilities due to HIV will most probably continue to climb because of increased access to antiretroviral therapy (ART) treatments, which extend the life expectancy of people with HIV but cannot cure them. On the other hand, new WHO guidelines which have increased the recommended CD4 count[2] at which to provide antiretroviral drug treatment are seen as an important evolution in reducing the incidence of disability among people living with HIV (Eaton et al., 2014).

East Africa's rapid urbanisation is shifting the incidence of poverty

Africa is urbanising fast: according to UN projections, Africa is expected to be 56% urban in 2050, versus 40% in 2014.[3] In 1990, Africa was the region of the world with the smallest urban population, at 197 million; by 2020, it will have the second-highest number after Asia (560 million versus 2.2 billion respectively) (AfDB, OECD and UNDP, 2016). Figure 1.11 shows historic and projected urban population growth in sub-Saharan Africa relative to North Africa and Latin America and the Caribbean. While Latin America's cities are expected to keep growing between now and 2050, the population in rural areas is projected to fall; Sub-Saharan Africa is the only region where rural populations will also show strong growth in the future.

Figure 1.11. **Urban and rural populations by region, 1950-2050**

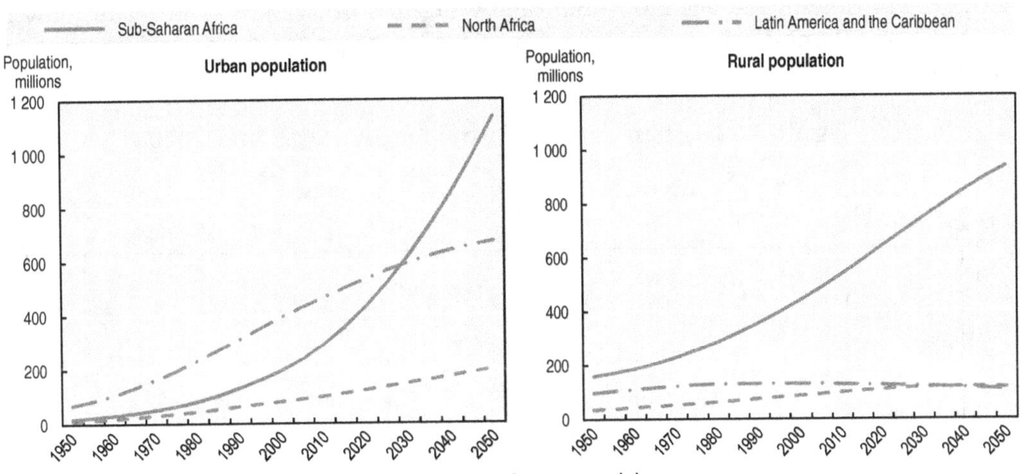

Source: UN DESA (2014), World Urbanization Prospects: The 2014 Revision.

East Africa is the least urbanised region in the world. Some 25.6% of the East African population lived in urban areas in 2015, the lowest level of any region globally and also significantly below Middle Africa (44.0%) and West Africa (45.1%). The global level of urbanisation was 54.0% in 2015. In that year, Ethiopia and Tanzania were the most urbanised of the sample countries, while Zambia and Mozambique were the least urbanised (Figure 1.12). However, this is partly attributable to different definitions of 'urban' across the countries.[4]

Figure 1.12. **The level and growth rate of urban populations across the sample countries - historic and projected**

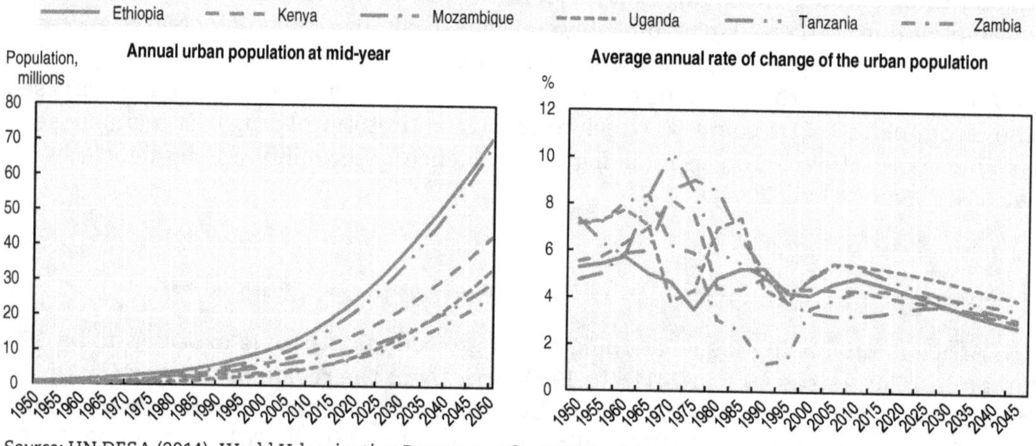

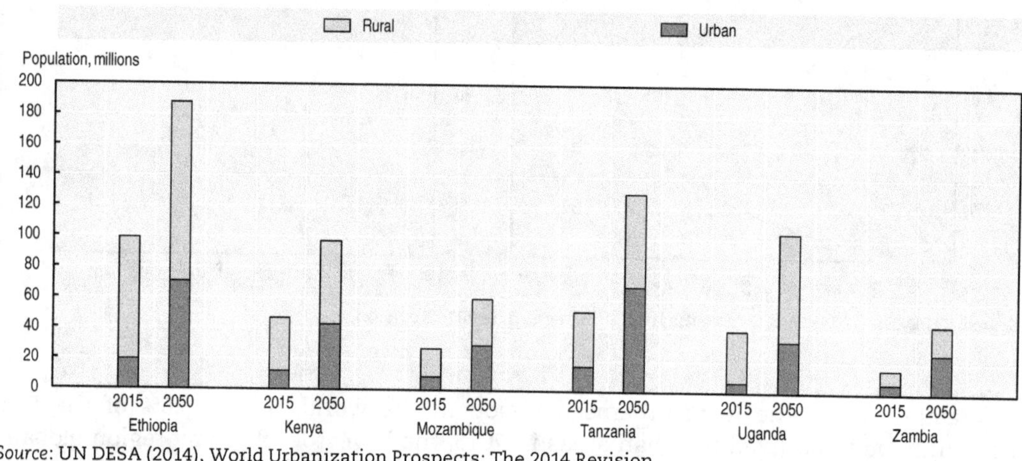

Source: UN DESA (2014), World Urbanization Prospects: The 2014 Revision.

There has been rapid growth in urban populations across the sample since 1950, most notably in the 1960s and 1970s (Figure 1.12). The UN expects rapid urbanisation to continue until at least 2050: according to its latest projections, urban populations will be more than three times higher in 2050 than in 2015 in Mozambique, Kenya and Ethiopia, more than four times higher in Zambia and Tanzania and more than five times higher in Uganda (UN DESA, 2014). Over the same period, rural populations will increase as well, with growth ranging between 47% in Ethiopia to 110% in Uganda. As a result, only in Tanzania and Zambia will the urban populations be larger than the rural populations by 2050 (Figure 1.13).

Figure 1.13. **Urban and rural populations, 2015 and 2050**

Source: UN DESA (2014), World Urbanization Prospects: The 2014 Revision.

As discussed in the 2016 African Economic Outlook, "Africa's urban growth has to a large extent taken the form of urban villages, diffusing urban growth in smaller towns" (AfDB, OECD and UNDP, 2016). These "urban villages" exist at the interface of rural and urban areas and are the residence of 82% of Africa's population. This form of urbanisation raises important challenges regarding infrastructure, governance and the provision of basic services in cities which, in certain cases, have not yet been built. The financial and administrative challenges associated with African urbanisation are likely to be immense. The blurring of urban and rural is reflected by the fact that about 40% of African urban dwellers are engaged in some form of agricultural activity (FAO, 2012). At the same time, rural livelihoods tend not to depend solely on agriculture, even in the least developed countries (UNCTAD, 2015).

Poverty in sub-Saharan Africa is often considered a predominantly rural problem: in 2012, the poverty rate in rural areas was 46%, versus 18% in urban areas, and the absolute number of poor people residing outside cities was far higher (Beegle et al., 2016). Higher levels of urbanisation are associated with lower poverty and higher GDP per capita globally (Kariuki et al., 2013), suggesting that the rapid pace of urbanisation in Africa will play an important role in accelerating the decline in poverty. Rural poverty rates are higher than urban rates across the six sample countries (Figure 1.14); the disparity is greatest in Zambia and smallest in Ethiopia and Mozambique.

Figure 1.14. **Poverty rate in urban versus rural areas**

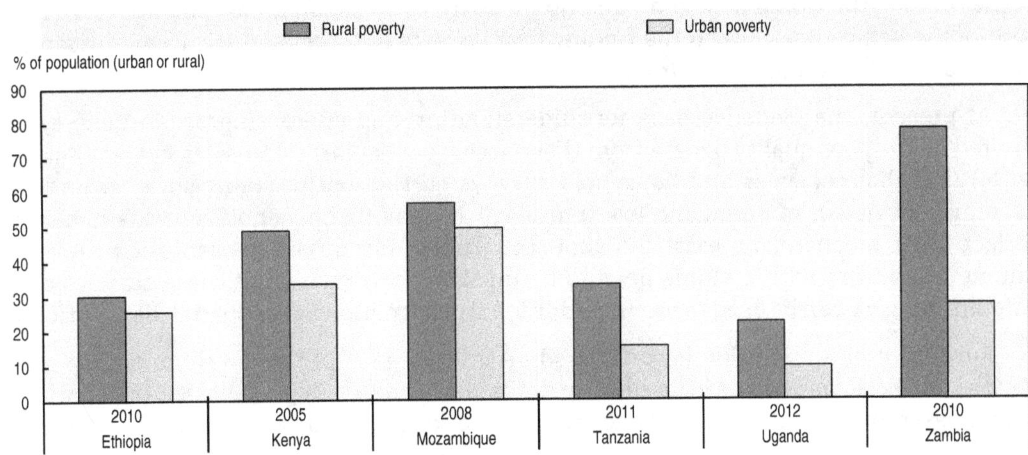

Source: World Bank (2016), World Development Indicators (database).

Yet urban poverty dynamics will evolve as the nature of African urbanisation changes. Ravaillon, Chen and Sangraula (2007) find that the urban share of countries' extreme poor is rising across the world, with the trend particularly pronounced in sub-Saharan Africa. A binary distinction between rural and urban is also not very instructive. As the World Bank and the IMF note (2013): "[P]eople and poverty are located along a continuous "settlement" spectrum ranging from sparsely populated rural areas, to small towns to small cities, to megacities". Outside Africa, urban poverty is lowest in the largest cities while the incidence of poverty and the total number of poor people is higher in smaller cities. In Africa, however, the urban poor are concentrated in the largest cities, in part because these currently account for such a large share of the total urban population. As Africa's smaller towns develop, it is possible that urban poverty trends in the region will converge with trends evident elsewhere in the world.

Some 55% of sub-Saharan Africa's urban population lived in large-scale informal settlements (slums) in 2014 – a decline from 70% in 1990 but still almost twice the level for the developing world as a whole (UN-Habitat, 2016). Five of the six sample countries exceeded this level: Mozambique registered the highest proportion (80.5%) and Kenya the lowest (54.7%) in 2015 (UN-Habitat, 2015). Urban poverty is concentrated in these areas: half of slum-dwellers live below the absolute poverty line (AfDB, OECD and UNDP, 2015). A defining characteristic of slums is the absence or poor quality of services, housing and infrastructure, implying that multi-dimensional poverty levels in such areas might be similar to rural areas. As the African Economic Outlook (AEO) 2015 notes, "the deprivations faced by the rural and urban poor are similar" (AfDB, OECD and UNDP, 2015). At the same time, there are major structural differences between urban and rural poverty. The cost of living is higher in urban areas and the seasonal dynamics of poverty are likely to differ (Kaminski, Christiaensen and Gilbert, 2014), while there is also likely to be greater pressure on shared services in urban areas.

Health outcomes in slums are a particular concern. Although infant and maternal mortality rates are typically significantly lower in urban areas than rural in sub-Saharan Africa, this does not hold in Tanzania, where infant, child and maternal mortality are higher in urban areas than rural (United Republic of Tanzania, 2015). It is likely that a similar tendency might exist in slum areas across the other sample countries (Olack et al., 2014). Urban residents are subject to a range of different health risks than rural dwellers, most notably air pollution. Moreover, incidence of HIV/AIDS differs between rural and urban areas: Magadi (2013) finds that the prevalence of HIV in sub-Saharan Africa is higher among the urban poor than among those living in urban areas who are relatively well-off, which contrasts with the finding that poverty is associated with a significantly lower rate of HIV infection in rural areas.

At present, the evidence base for understanding and addressing urban poverty is limited by the poor quality of data from these areas, particularly slums. Lucci and Bhatkal (2014) find that censuses and household surveys carried out in slums suffer from low coverage, low levels of detail and low frequency. Improving household surveys to better reflect what mechanisms exist for poor and vulnerable urban residents is required. Enumerators from within slums need to be involved in carrying out these surveys and satellite imagery can be used to provide additional information about spatial distributions.

Rural-to-urban migration is considered an integral part of the development process (Lewis, 1954): surplus labour in rural areas is attracted by higher wages paid by the urban-based industrial sector. By encouraging working-age household members to find higher-paid work in towns and cities, rural households diversify income sources and can offset localised economic shocks. Remittances also enable recipient families to hold more productive capital and are thus a means of overcoming capital market imperfections (Rutaremwa, 2011). However, migration fragments households, diminishing the capacity of its members to pool income and care for each other. This undermines the role that households and social networks can play in providing informal support and is creating space and demand for formal, public social protection arrangements.

The dynamics of future migration flows are uncertain

The UN population projections used in this study do not anticipate migration to be a major determinant of population change in the sample countries. They expect net emigration across the six countries between 2015 and 2065 of a modest size.[5] In terms of annual rates per 1 000 home population, Tanzania and Uganda are projected to have the largest net emigration over the 50-year period, followed by Zambia. The projected rates for Kenya, Mozambique and Ethiopia are very low, at less than 1 in 5 000 each year. The implication is net emigration of just under 5 million from the six countries in the next 50 years, and just under 8.5 million from East Africa as a whole. By way of comparison, more than 40 million people moved from Europe to the "New World" between 1850 and 1913.

Intra-African migration could exacerbate the population boom in the six sample countries. Movement between countries within sub-Saharan Africa accounts for almost 65% of migration in the region (World Bank, 2011). This movement is most often linked to the search for employment but might also relate to the vagaries of state formation that cut across ethnic boundaries or are driven by conflict and political unrest. There exists significant movement between the sample countries, with migration channels identified from Zambia to Tanzania, Uganda to Kenya and Tanzania to Kenya. Tanzania is also a favoured destination for migrants from the Democratic Republic of Congo and Burundi. Conflict or climate change could lead to significant movement of people between the six sample countries or net immigration to the six sample countries from neighbouring states in East and Middle Africa.

The very low level of emigration projected by the UN is based on an extrapolation of existing trends. It appears very conservative given the unprecedented rate of population growth across the sample countries. Between 2005 and 2050, the number of individuals aged 15-39 (the cohort most likely to emigrate) is projected to rise by 176 million, an increase of 316%. Assuming constant average labour force participation rates across the six countries (at 80% on average), a higher bound estimate of the surplus labour or potential supply of migrants from East Africa could stand at 140 million. The negative impact of population growth in terms of employment availability and incomes might serve as a significant push factor for migration, compounding the incentive to migrate associated with the better living standards potentially available in wealthier countries. At the same time, the demographic trends of wealthier countries are likely to serve as a pull factor: population ageing is projected to reduce the size of the economically active working age population in 25 Western European states and territories by 66.3 million between 2005 and 2050 (Koettl, 2010). This reduction is expected to be sharpest during the period 2010-30.

Koettl (2010) describes the disparity in population trends between low- and high-income countries as an opportunity for "demographic arbitrage", which benefits both the receiving nations (by increasing the size of their workforce) and the sending nations (by alleviating pressure on their own labour markets and reducing the possibility of an ageing crisis once the youth bulge reaches retirement). Relative to other regions in sub-Saharan Africa, East African migrants are more likely to leave the continent and thus take advantage of this opportunity: according to World Bank data, 41% of East African migrants leave Africa, versus 24% from West Africa, 39% from Middle Africa and 28% from Southern Africa (World Bank, 2011). However, this arbitrage is reliant not only on policies within Europe that allow for the large-scale movement of labour but also on migrants possessing the type and level of skills required by the receiving countries.

Climate change poses a massive threat to livelihoods

Africa is the continent most vulnerable to climate change. Current models indicate that climate change will affect both temperatures and rainfall levels in East Africa. According to the International Food Policy Research Institute, temperatures in the region will increase by between 1.3°C and 2.1°C by 2050 while rainfall will either increase or remain the same across the region on average but might decrease significantly in Ethiopia (IFPRI, 2013). East Africa will also be vulnerable to the extreme weather events associated with climate change such as droughts and flooding that have a much faster impact.

Climate change has been overwhelmingly driven by emissions from high-income countries yet its consequences are overwhelmingly endured by low-income countries. Africa's population growth has been a relatively minor contributor to climate change so far but this is likely to change over the next 50 years. As economies in the region grow wealthier and consumption rises, so too will emissions. The growth of cities and a shift away from agriculture towards industry are likely to compound this effect. Moreover, population pressures will reduce the region's resilience to climate change through a number of channels.

Deforestation and over-grazing, both closely associated to the challenge of feeding rapidly-growing populations, result in soil erosion and desertification, both of which render land unproductive over time and reduce its resilience to climate shocks (Stephenson, Newman and Mayhew, 2010). East Africa's Lake Victoria is not only shrinking as a result of climate change, but it is also suffering from a rapid loss in biodiversity as a result of pollution and over-fishing; its ability to sustain livelihoods and to provide food for neighbouring countries is diminishing.

The impact of climate change will not only be felt inland. Sea-level rises and associated coastal erosion are a major concern for residents of coastal areas in Kenya, Tanzania and Mozambique. Mozambique is also highly vulnerable to tropical cyclones, which are linked to increases in water temperatures associated with climate change. The consequences of climate change in coastal areas affect not only economic activities in these areas but also diminish the natural defences that protect inland areas from the impact of rising sea levels. On a regional level, the damage inflicted on both inland and coastal areas risks instigating large-scale migration crises.

East Africa's capacity to feed itself and meet its needs in terms of water provision will be further strained. East Africa is already one of the most food insecure regions in the world: 28% of the population suffered severe malnutrition in 2014/15 versus an average of 26% for sub-Saharan Africa as a whole. Some 44% of children in Eastern Africa are stunted, the highest proportion in Africa (FAO, 2017). The World Food Programme's hunger and climate vulnerability index classifies vulnerability in these dimensions to be very high in Mozambique, Kenya and Ethiopia and high in the other sample countries (WFP, 2015).

These challenges are likely to be exacerbated by rapid population growth and by the urbanisation projected for the period ahead. Urbanisation is typically associated with higher demand for food, which puts greater strain on domestic agricultural production (AfDB, OECD and UNDP, 2016).

Climate change will cause acute shocks (in the form of natural disasters) and a gradual deterioration of conditions both in-land and in coastal areas. In both cases, poor households are the most vulnerable, and the adverse impacts can be long-lasting: Ethiopian households that suffered during the 1984/85 drought continued to experience 2-3% less annual per capita income growth in the 1990s (del Ninno, Coll-Black and Fallavier, 2016).

Hallegatte et al. (2017) identify five reasons why poor households are disproportionately affected by natural disasters: i) overexposure (poor households are more likely to live in areas or accommodation susceptible to regular events such as floods); ii) higher vulnerability (poor households typically suffer higher losses when natural disasters strike); iii) lower ability to cope and recover after an event (due largely to a lack of public support); iv) permanent impacts on education and health (a result of negative coping strategies); and v) *ex ante* changes to behaviour (vulnerability to natural disasters deters poor households from investing in livelihoods). Over the longer term, poor households are less able to move or diversify their livelihoods in response to deterioration in their livelihoods resulting from climate change.

Climate change affects the key determinants of health: access to clean air, food and safe drinking water and shelter. Its negative health impacts include the proliferation of communicable diseases: according to the World Health Organization, between 2030 and 2050, it is expected to cause approximately 250 000 additional deaths per year worldwide, from malnutrition, malaria, diarrhoea and heat stress (WHO, 2016). Given the heightened impact in sub-Saharan Africa and the fact that low-income countries are least able to mitigate these adverse health impacts, climate change will place East Africa's public health services under severe strain.

Notes

1. The fertility transition refers to the decline in fertility from an average level of four or more children per woman to an average of 2.1 children per woman, which is known as "replacement level" and is generally accepted to be the level of fertility required to keep their population constant (absent migration). Oppenheim Mason (1997) provides a useful summary of the historical literature on fertility.

2. CD4 stands for *cluster of differentiation* 4 and is used to identify the number of a certain type of white blood cells which are depleted in the blood by the virus. The lower the level of CD4 count, the weaker is the immune system of the patient.

3. The figures quoted in this section come from the United Nations Department of Economic and Social Affairs *World Urbanization Prospects, 2014 Revision*. The population data are not strictly comparable with the 2015 *World Population Prospects* revisions but the discrepancy is not sufficient to undermine the validity of the urbanisation projections.

4. The United Nations *World Urbanization Prospects, 2014 revision* uses the same definition of 'urban' as each country uses (summarised in Annex 1.A3); among the six sample countries, no two definitions are the same, which makes cross-country comparisons of urbanization difficult.

5. Information on the six countries is set out in Annex 1.A1.

References

AfDB, OECD and UNDP (2016), *African Economic Outlook 2016: Sustainable Cities and Structural Transformation*, OECD Publishing, Paris, http://dx.doi.org/10.1787/aeo-2016-en.

AfDB, OECD and UNDP (2015), *African Economic Outlook 2015: Regional Development and Spatial Inclusion*, OECD Publishing, Paris, http://dx.doi.org/10.1787/aeo-2015-en.

Beegle, K. et al. (2016), *Poverty in a Rising Africa*, World Bank, Washington, DC, http://dx.doi.org/10.1596/978-1-4648-0723-7.

Bongaarts, J. (2008), "Fertility Transitions in Developing Countries: Progress or Stagnation?", *Studies in Family Planning* 39(2), pp. 105-10, ncbi.nlm.nih.gov/pubmed/18678174.

Cleland, J. (2006), "Family planning: the unfinished agenda", *The Lancet* 368(9549), pp. 18–24, http://dx.doi.org/10.1016/S0140-6736(06)69480-4.

del Ninno, C., S. Coll-Black and P. Fallavier (2016), *Social Protection Programs for Africa's Drylands*, World Bank Studies, Washington, DC, http://dx.doi.org/10.1596/978-1-4648-0846-3.

Dye, C. (2014), "After 2015: Infectious diseases in a new era of health and development," *The Royal Society Publishing* 369(1645), http://dx.doi.org/10.1098/rstb.2013.0426.

Eaton, J.W. et al. (2014), "Health benefits, costs, and cost-effectiveness of earlier eligibility for adult antiretroviral therapy and expanded treatment coverage: a combined analysis of 12 mathematical models," *The Lancet* 2(1): 23–34.

Ezeh, A.C., B.U. Mberu and J.O. Emina (2009), "Stall in fertility decline in Eastern African countries: regional analysis of patterns, determinants and implications," *The Royal Society Publishing* 364(1532), http://dx.doi.org/10.1098/rstb.2009.0166.

FAO (2017), *Regional overview of food security and nutrition: the challenges of building resilience to shocks and stresses*, Food and Agricultural Organisation, Accra.

FAO (2012), *Growing Greener Cities in Africa*, Food and Agriculture Organization, Rome.

FAO, IFAD, WFP (2015), *The State of Food Insecurity in the World*, Food and Agriculture Organization, International Fund for Agricultural Development and the World Food Programme.

Federal Democratic Republic of Ethiopia (2014), *Population Stabilization Report*, Addis Ababa.

Foster, V. and C. Briceño-Garmendia (2010), *Africa's infrastructure: a time for transformation*, World Bank, Washington, DC, openknowledge.worldbank.org/handle/10986/2692.

Goujon, A., W. Lutz and S. KC (2015), "Education stalls and subsequent stalls in African fertility: A descriptive overview", *Demographic Research* 33(47), pp. 1281-1296, http://dx.doi.org/10.4054/DemRes.2015.33.47.

Hallegatte, S. et al. (2017), *Unbreakable: Building the Resilience of the Poor in the Face of Natural Disasters*, World Bank, Washington, DC, openknowledge.worldbank.org/handle/10986/25335.

IFPRI (2013), *East African Agriculture and Climate Change: A Comprehensive Analysis*, International Food Policy Research Institute.

ILO (2015), *Global Employment Trends for Youth 2015: Scaling up investments in decent jobs for youth*, World Health Organization, Geneva.

Kaminski, J., L. Christiaensen and C.L. Gilbert (2014), "The End of Seasonality? New Insights from Sub-Saharan Africa", *Policy Research Working Paper*, No. 6907, World Bank, Washington, DC, https://openknowledge.worldbank.org/handle/10986/18771.

Kariuki, R.M. et al. (2013), *Harnessing urbanization to end poverty and boost prosperity in Africa: an action agenda for transformation*, World Bank, Washington, DC.

Koettl, J. (2010), "Prospects for Management of Migration between Europe and the Middle East and North Africa", World Bank, Middle East and North Africa Region, Poverty Reduction and Economic Management Network, Washington, DC.

Lewis, W.A. (1954), "Economic Development with Unlimited Supplies of Labour", *The Manchester School* 22, pp. 139–191, http://dx.doi.org/10.1111/j.1467-9957.1954.tb00021.x.

Lucci, P. and T. Bhatkal (2014), "Monitoring progress on urban poverty: are current data and indicators fit for purpose?", Overseas Development Institute, London.

Machiyama, K. (2010), "A Re-examination of Recent Fertility Declines in Sub-Saharan Africa", *DHS Working Papers Series*, No. 68.

Magadi, M.A. (2013), "The disproportionate high risk of HIV infection among the urban poor in sub-Saharan Africa", *AIDS Behav* 17(5), pp.1645-1654, http://dx.doi.org/10.1007/s10461-012-0217-y.

Muhoza, D.N., A. Broekhuis and P. Hooimeijer (2014), "Variations in Desired Family Size and Excess Fertility in East Africa", *International Journal of Population Research*, http://dx.doi.org/10.1155/2014/486079.

Olack, B. et al. (2014), "Mortality Trends Observed in Population-Based Surveillance of an Urban Slum Settlement, Kibera, Kenya, 2007–2010", *PLOS ONE* 9(1), pp. 1-6, http://dx.doi.org/10.1371/journal.pone.0085913.

Oppenheim Mason, K. (1997), "Explaining Fertility Transitions", *Demography* 34(4), pp. 443-454, jstor.org/stable/3038299.

Ravallion, M., S. Chen and P. Sangraula (2007), "New evidence on the urbanization of global poverty", *Policy Research Working Paper*, No. 4199, World Bank, Washington, DC, http://dx.doi. org/10.1596/1813-9450-4199.

Republic of Kenya (2012), *National Population Policy*, Republic of Kenya, Nairobi.

Republic of Kenya (1986), *National Population Policyy*, Republic of Kenya, Nairobi.

Republic of Kenya (1967), *National Population Policy*, Republic of Kenya, Nairobi.

Republic of Mozambique (1999), *National Population Policy*, Republic of Mozambique, Maputo.

Republic of Uganda (2011), *National Population Policy*, Republic of Uganda, Kampala.

Republic of Uganda (2008), *National Population Policy*, Republic of Uganda, Kampala.

Republic of Uganda (1995), *National Population Policy*, Republic of Uganda, Kampala.

Republic of Zambia (2007), *National Population Policy*, Republic of Zambia, Lusaka.

Republic of Zambia (1989), *National Population Policy*, Republic of Zambia, Lusaka.

Rutaremwa, G. (2011), "Impact of internal and international migration: the East African experience," *Working Paper* No. 20, RMMRU, Dhaka.

Stephenson, J., K. Newman and S. Mayhew (2010), "Population dynamics and climate change: what are the links?", *Oxford Journal of Public Health* 32(2), pp. 150-156, https://dx.doi.org/10.1093/ pubmed/fdq038.

Transitional Government of Ethiopia (1993), *National Population Policy*, Transitional Government of Ethiopia, Addis Ababa.

UN DESA (2015a), *World Population Prospects: The 2015 Revision*, United Nations Department of Economic and Social Affairs, New York.

UN DESA (2015b), *World Population Prospects: The 2015 Revision Methodology of the United Nations Population Estimates and Projections*, ESA/P/WP.242, United Nations Department of Economic and Social Affairs, New York.

UN DESA (2014), *World Urbanization Prospects: The 2014 Revision*, United Nations Department of Economic and Social Affairs, New York.

UN-Habitat (2016), *World Cities Report 2016: Urbanization and Development – Emerging Futures*, United Nations Human Settlements Programme, Nairobi.

UN-Habitat (2015), *UN-Habitat Urban Data* (database), accessed February 2017, urbandata.unhabitat. org.

UNCTAD (2015), "Economic Diversification, Non-Farm Activities and Rural Transformation", in *The Least Developed Countries Report: Transforming Rural Economies*, United Nations Conference on Trade and Development, Geneva, pp. 77 – 110, http://unctad.org/en/PublicationsLibrary/ ldc2015_en.pdf.

UNICEF/WHO (2015), *Progress on sanitation and drinking water: 2015 update and MDG assessment*, United Nations Children's Fund and World Health Organization.

United Republic of Tanzania (2015), "Mortality and Health", National Bureau of Statistics, Ministry of Finance, Office of Chief Government Statistician, Ministry of State, United Republic of Tanzania, Dar es Salaam.

United Republic of Tanzania (2006), *National Population Policy*, United Republic of Tanzania, Dodoma.

United Republic of Tanzania (1992), *National Population Policy*, United Republic of Tanzania, Dodoma.

USAID (2012), *Three Successful Sub-Saharan Africa Family Planning Programs: Lessons for Meeting the MDGs*, USAID/Africa Bureau, USAID/Population and Reproductive Health, Ethiopia Federal Ministry of Health, Malawi Ministry of Health, Rwanda Ministry of Health.

WFP (2015), *Food Insecurity & Climate Change*, World Food Programme, Rome.

WHO (2016), "Climate change and health", fact sheet, World Health Organisation, Geneva, who.int/ mediacentre/factsheets/fs266/en.

World Bank (2016), *World Development Indicators* (database), accessed October 2016, http://data. worldbank.org/products/wdi.

World Bank (2015), *World Development Indicators* (database), accessed June 2015, http://data. worldbank.org/products/wdi.

World Bank (2011), *Leveraging Migration for Africa: Remittances, Skills, and Investments*, World Bank, Washington DC.

World Bank and IMF (2013), *Global Monitoring Report 2013: Rural-Urban Dynamics and the Millennium Development Goals*, World Bank and International Monetary Fund, Washington, DC, openknowledge.worldbank.org/handle/10986/13330.

Annex 1.A1. Net migration into the six countries

In the UN WPP methodology manual, it is noted that:

"In preparing assumptions about future trends in international migration, several pieces of information were taken into account: (1) information on net international migration or its components (immigration and emigration) as recorded by countries; (2) data on labour migration flows; (3) estimates of undocumented or irregular migration; (4) and data on refugee movements in recent periods… Given the lack of suitable information on the age distribution of migrant flows, models were generally used to distribute the overall net number of male and female migrants by age group according to the dominant type of migration flow assumed… As a final step, it was necessary to ensure that the sum of all international migration added to zero at the global level for each 5-year estimation and projection period. This was achieved by an iterative process in which individual country estimates and projections were revisited and altered accordingly".

Net migration is the inflow of immigrants minus the outflow of emigrants. A positive number reflects a net inflow and a negative number a net outflow. The absolute number of migrants is shown in 10-year intervals as is the migration rate, expressed as the annual net number of migrants per thousand of the home population. The numbers for immigrants and emigrants are not published separately (UN DESA, 2015b).

Table 1.A1.1. Net migration flows, in thousands of people

Country	2015-25	2025-35	2035-45	2045-55	2055-65
Ethiopia	-120	-120	-120	-117	-105
Kenya	-100	-100	-100	-98	-88
Mozambique	-50	-50	-50	-49	-44
Tanzania	-400	-400	-400	-390	-350
Uganda	-300	-300	-300	-293	-263
Zambia	-80	-50	-50	-49	-44

Source: UN DESA (2015a), World Population Prospects: The 2015 Revision.

Table 1.A1.2. Rates, per thousand of the population

Country	2015-25	2025-35	2035-45	2045-55	2055-65
Ethiopia	-0.11	-0.09	-0.07	-0.06	-0.05
Kenya	-0.19	-0.15	-0.13	-0.1	-0.08
Mozambique	-0.16	-0.12	-0.09	-0.07	-0.06
Tanzania	-0.66	-0.49	-0.37	-0.29	-0.21
Uganda	-0.64	-0.48	-0.37	-0.29	-0.21
Zambia	-0.42	-0.2	-0.15	-0.11	-0.08

Source: UN DESA (2015a), World Population Prospects: The 2015 Revision.

References

UN DESA (2015a), *World Population Prospects: The 2015 Revision*, United Nations Department of Economic and Social Affairs, New York.

UN DESA (2015b), *World Population Prospects: The 2015 Revision Methodology of the United Nations Population Estimates and Projections*, Report ESA/P/WP.242, United Nations Department of Economic and Social Affairs, Population Division.

Annex 1.A2. HIV/AIDS

Table 1.A2.1. HIV/AIDS

Country	Year	AIDS deaths	HIV prevalence	AIDS YLD as a per cent of all YLD	
			aged 15-49	aged 15-29 (%)	aged 30-59 (%)
Ethiopia	2001	110 000	3.9		
Ethiopia	2005	120 000	2.6		
Ethiopia	2009	72 000	1.6		
Ethiopia	2012			0.6	1.6
Ethiopia	2013	45 000	1.2		
Kenya	2001	170 000	8.7		
Kenya	2005	150 000	6.6		
Kenya	2009	86 000	6.0		
Kenya	2012			3.5	8.3
Kenya	2013	58 000	6.0		
Mozambique	2001	39 000	8.8		
Mozambique	2005	73 000	11.1		
Mozambique	2009	72 000	11.3		
Mozambique	2012			5.0	12.1
Mozambique	2013	82 000	10.8		
Tanzania	2001	130 000	7.9		
Tanzania	2005	140 000	6.6		
Tanzania	2009	95 000	5.7		
Tanzania	2012			2.7	6.9
Tanzania	2013	78 000	5.0		
Uganda	2001	100 000	6.8		
Uganda	2005	78 000	6.2		
Uganda	2009	66 000	6.8		
Uganda	2012			3.0	7.9
Uganda	2013	63 000	7.4		
Zambia	2001	74 000	14.4		
Zambia	2005	68 000	13.7		
Zambia	2009	34 000	13.2		
Zambia	2012			5.0	12.5
Zambia	2013	27 000	12.5		

Source: WHO, Health Statistics and Information Systems.

Annex 1.A3. National definitions of urban, East African countries

Country	Last census	Definition
Ethiopia	2012	Localities with 2 000 inhabitants or more.
Kenya	2009	Municipalities, town councils, and other urban centres with 2 000 inhabitants or more. Due to substantial changes in the 1999 census delineations of urban areas, only the population for the "urban core" is considered to ensure consistency with previous censuses.
Mozambique	2007	In the 1997 and 2007 censuses: 23 cities and 68 towns/vilas.
Tanzania	2012	Urban areas are defined using several criteria and include all regional and district headquarters, as well as all wards with urban characteristics (i.e. exceeding certain minimal level of size-density criteria and/or with many of their inhabitants in non-agricultural occupations). No specific numerical values of size and density are identified, and wards are defined as urban based on the decision of the District/Regional Census Committees.
Uganda	2011	Gazetted cities, municipalities and towns with 2 000 inhabitants or more.
Zambia	2010	Localities of 5 000 inhabitants or more, with a majority of the labour force not in agricultural activities.

Chapter 2

Forecasting economic and social trends for long-term social protection planning

Identifying how Africa's population boom will interact with key socio-economic trends is crucial to understanding the evolving needs for social protection and the context within which it will operate. This chapter forecasts economic and social trends of key interest to social protection planners in the sample countries. It estimates the rate at which these economies and their per capita incomes will grow, as well as the impact this growth will have on poverty. It also projects the structure of the economy and the labour force in order to show how workers are likely to be employed over the next 50 years.

The prospects for growth are strong in East Africa

Economic growth rates across the six countries have improved markedly since the 2000s after stagnating during the 1980s and 1990s (Figure 2.1). East Africa outperformed sub-Saharan Africa as a whole between 2000 and 2015 and is expected to do so over the next five years. The strong economic growth witnessed since the early 2000s has increased per capita incomes (Figure 2.2).[1] However, population growth has diluted this impact such that only Zambia and Kenya have graduated to middle income status (as determined by World Bank thresholds). This in turn has slowed the rate of poverty reduction, an effect exacerbated by the level of inequality across the six countries. Despite their strong economic performance in recent years, all the sample countries with the exception of Kenya are still classified by the United Nations as Least Developed Countries.

Figure 2.1. **Average GDP growth rates, historic and projected, 1980-2020**

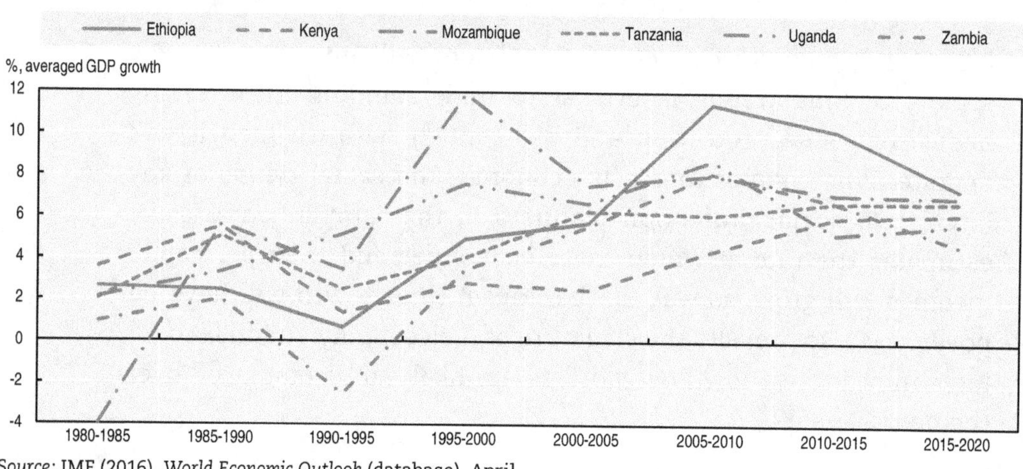

Source: IMF (2016), *World Economic Outlook* (database), April.

Beyond 2020, much will depend on the countries' capacity to improve infrastructure. Investment in infrastructure has been a major contributor to the African growth story in recent years (Foster and Briceño-Garmendia, 2010) but has not been nearly sufficient to meet the region's deficit in this regard relative to the rest of the world. Sustained and high levels of investment will rely on the countries' capacity to mobilise savings and attract foreign investment.

Domestic savings across the sample vary, both in terms of level and trend. Ethiopia's gross domestic savings rate has grown strongly since 2010, reaching 31.8% of GDP in 2015. Kenya's gross domestic savings rate, on the other hand, has declined from 17.3% of GDP in 2007 to 12.7% in 2015. The trend since 2010 has been flat in Tanzania and Uganda at just above 20% of GDP. The average gross domestic savings rate for sub-Saharan Africa as a whole was 15.4% of GDP in 2015, versus 17.3% of GDP in Latin America and the Caribbean and 29.6% of GDP in Emerging Asia. Investment rates across the six countries have been higher than the savings rate (dramatically so, in Mozambique's case), meaning that the countries have been able to attract foreign investment to fill this financing gap (IMF, 2016).

It is not advisable to extrapolate current economic trends far into the future; past performance is no guarantee of future outcomes. Easterly et al. (1993), for example, demonstrated that growth rates are unstable over time, with correlations across decades of 0.1 to 0.3, even though country characteristics are much more stable. This cautions against projecting forward the growth rates achieved in the last 15 years. In terms of the future, the long-term economic prospects not only of sub-Saharan Africa but also of the world as a whole are laden with uncertainty. The projections used in this report should not be regarded as predictions but as a means of understanding the interactions between different components of the economy.

Figure 2.2. **GNI per capita, 2015 USD (Atlas method, log scale)**

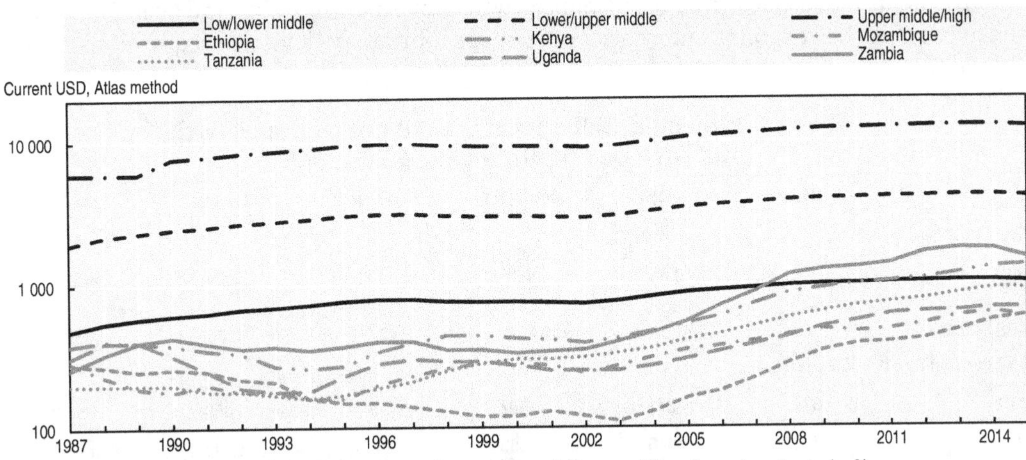

Source: World Bank (2016), *World Development Indicators,* http://data.worldbank.org/products/wdi.

The OECD long-term forecast of global GDP implies an annual growth rate of 2.53% from 2020 to 2065 (OECD, 2016). The United Nations' projections of the global population aged 15-64 implies an annual growth rate of 0.54% per annum. Assuming a constant employment rate, the OECD forecast implies that labour productivity will increase by 1.98% per year, which is slightly faster than the annual productivity growth rate of 1.8% found for the period 1965-2015 by the McKinsey Global Institute (2015). As the basis for the calculations in this chapter, a rate of productivity growth of three-quarters of the mean of the OECD projection and the McKinsey historical estimate is assumed for the six countries. This results in a projected increase in labour productivity of 1.4% per annum across the survey period. This is lower than the 2.2% found by McMillan and Harttgen (2014) for the 2000-10 period in 19 countries in sub-Saharan Africa.

Structural change – the process by which economic activity and employment typically move from agriculture (the primary sector) to industry and services (secondary and tertiary sectors) – has not been a major driver of development in sub-Saharan Africa. The region's secondary sector is dominated by extractive industries: manufacturing's share of GDP has declined from around 17% in the early 1990s to around 11% currently (versus 20% for extractive industries), raising the possibility that the region is already deindustrialising – a phenomenon typically associated with advanced economies (Page, 2013; Rodrik, 2015). Manufacturing is more labour-intensive than extractive industry and has proven much better at absorbing low-skilled labour. However, automation could jeopardise the employment gains associated with manufacturing growth in the future and is also likely to negatively impact employment generation in the services sector (Rodrik, 2015).

Even where structural transformation has taken place in Africa, the shift has been more from agriculture to services, where productivity growth has been low (de Vries et al., 2013). McMillan, Rodrik and Verduzco-Gallo (2014) find that since 1990, structural change has had a negative impact on growth in sub-Saharan Africa, though the picture has improved since 2000. Of course, the experience varies by country and will continue to do so: as noted by the AEO (AfDB, OECD and UNDP, 2015): "Countries are achieving growth with different degrees of sectoral transformation. In Ethiopia, structural changes are most pronounced with the share of agriculture in GDP shrinking (although remaining higher than in the other countries) and services expanding more than in the other countries."

Structural change is not just about economic output. Urbanisation and changes to the age structure of the population can transform societies and have been shown to promote productivity gains. Sub-Saharan Africa is in a position to capitalise from all three, in which case the projections in this Chapter will prove pessimistic. However, in none of these cases is the response automatic: rather, appropriate policies are required to exploit this potential.

Table 2.1. Projected GNP growth, GNP per capita growth, and GNP per capita levels, 2015-2065

	Ethiopia	Kenya	Mozambique	Tanzania	Uganda	Zambia
Average annual growth in:						
GDP	3.6%	3.5%	4.8%	4.3%	4.6%	4.6%
GDP per capita	2.0%	1.6%	2.5%	1.8%	2.0%	1.8%
GNP per capita (2015 US dollars):						
2015	634	1 371	607	864	639	1 509
2065	1 722	3 046	2 083	2 077	1 735	3 787

Source: Authors' calculations based on IMF (2015), IMF World Economic Outlook (database), October, and UN DESA (2015), World Population Prospects: The 2015 Revision.

Table 2.1 shows the growth in GDP, per capita GDP and GNP between 2015 and 2065 based on the assumed growth in productivity. The median GDP growth rate across the six countries over the projection period is 4.4% and 1.9% in per capita terms, which is close to the 2% projected by Rodrik (2014). Figure 2.3 shows the variation in average GDP growth rates across the six countries, which is a consequence of the differing growth rates of the working-age population relative to the total population across the sample countries. It also shows how population growth dilutes economy-wide gains on a per capita basis.

Figure 2.3. **Average annual GDP growth rates between 2015 and 2065**

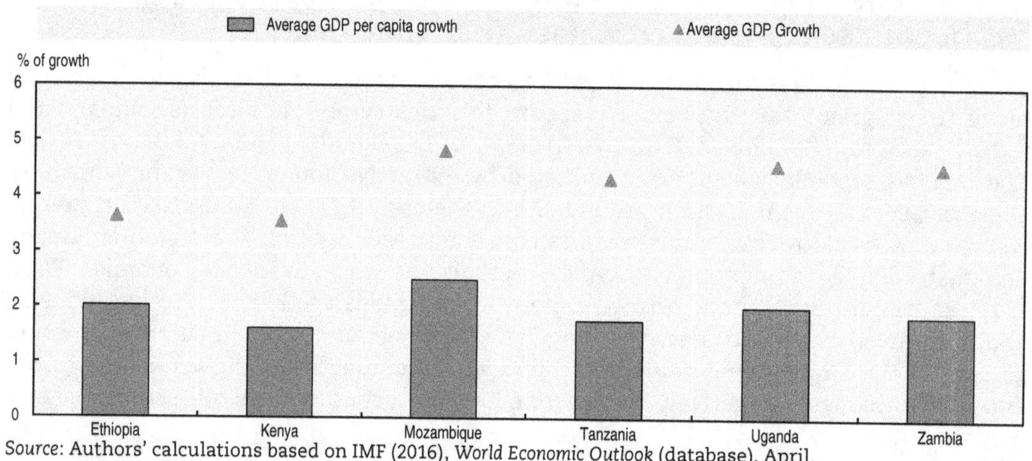

Source: Authors' calculations based on IMF (2016), *World Economic Outlook* (database), April.

A demographic dividend is represented by the excess of GDP per capita growth over the 1.4% assumed labour productivity growth. Ethiopia's annual average GDP growth rate is projected to be the second-slowest of the sample after Kenya but, because of its relatively slow population growth, its GDP per capita will grow by 2.0% per year on average, the second-fastest rate after Mozambique.

Slow structural change and the implications for employment

The next step is to show how the different sectors of the economy are likely to develop given the overall growth rates identified above. Figure 2.4 shows how the structure of output changed in the six countries between 2000 and 2010 and projects the composition of output by sector for 2065 based on the current trajectory as per the methodology applied by Fox et al. (2013). In all countries, the contribution of agriculture is projected to decline while that of services and industry increases. However, the contribution of agriculture is not projected to fall below half of its 2010 level in any of the six countries.

Figure 2.4. **Structure of output, 2000, 2010 and 2065**

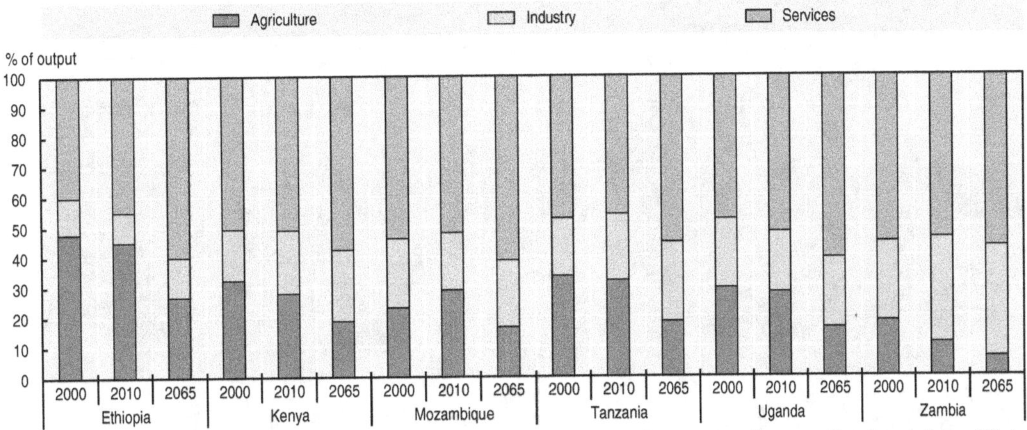

Source: Authors' calculations based on World Bank (2015), World Development Indicators (database), http://data.worldbank.org/products/wdi.

Having projected the structure of output, it is then possible to project the structure of employment up to 2065 across the three sectors, distinguishing between wage and non-wage employment in industry and services as per Fox's methodology. Figure 2.5 shows the results of this projection for each of the sample countries, which is based on three key assumptions: that labour force participation will remain at its present level, that the agricultural sector will absorb all employed people not absorbed by industry and services, and that the elasticity of employment for different sectors remains the same into the future. Partly because the agriculture sector is used to clear the market, it is projected to remain the majority form of employment in all countries in 2065, despite its declining contribution to output. Only in Tanzania and Zambia will agriculture account for less than 60% of employment at that point.

While wage employment in industry and services will increase as a proportion of total employment, it is projected to remain as a minority form of employment across this timeframe. Wage employment will be lower than employment in agriculture in all six countries and also lower than employment in household enterprises in Ethiopia, Tanzania and Uganda. A sensitivity analysis for these calculations (Annex 2.A1) indicates that agricultural and other informal work will remain predominant even under a more favourable development trajectory.

Figure 2.6 shows how new entrants to the labour market will be allocated across the labour market given the current absorption rates of different sectors. It indicates that 46% of the employment increase between 2015 and 2065 in the six countries together is projected to take place in agriculture, 28% in household enterprises, 20% in wage services and 6% in wage industry. If the labour force participation rate is to stay the same in each of the countries, additions to employment will need to total just over 7 million on average each year across the sample over the whole period. The projected demand for employment per year will vary over time in accordance with the trends in population growth, meaning it will rise relatively fast over the first 20 years of the timeframe before plateauing and then declining.

Figure 2.5. Employment shares by sector, 2010 and 2065

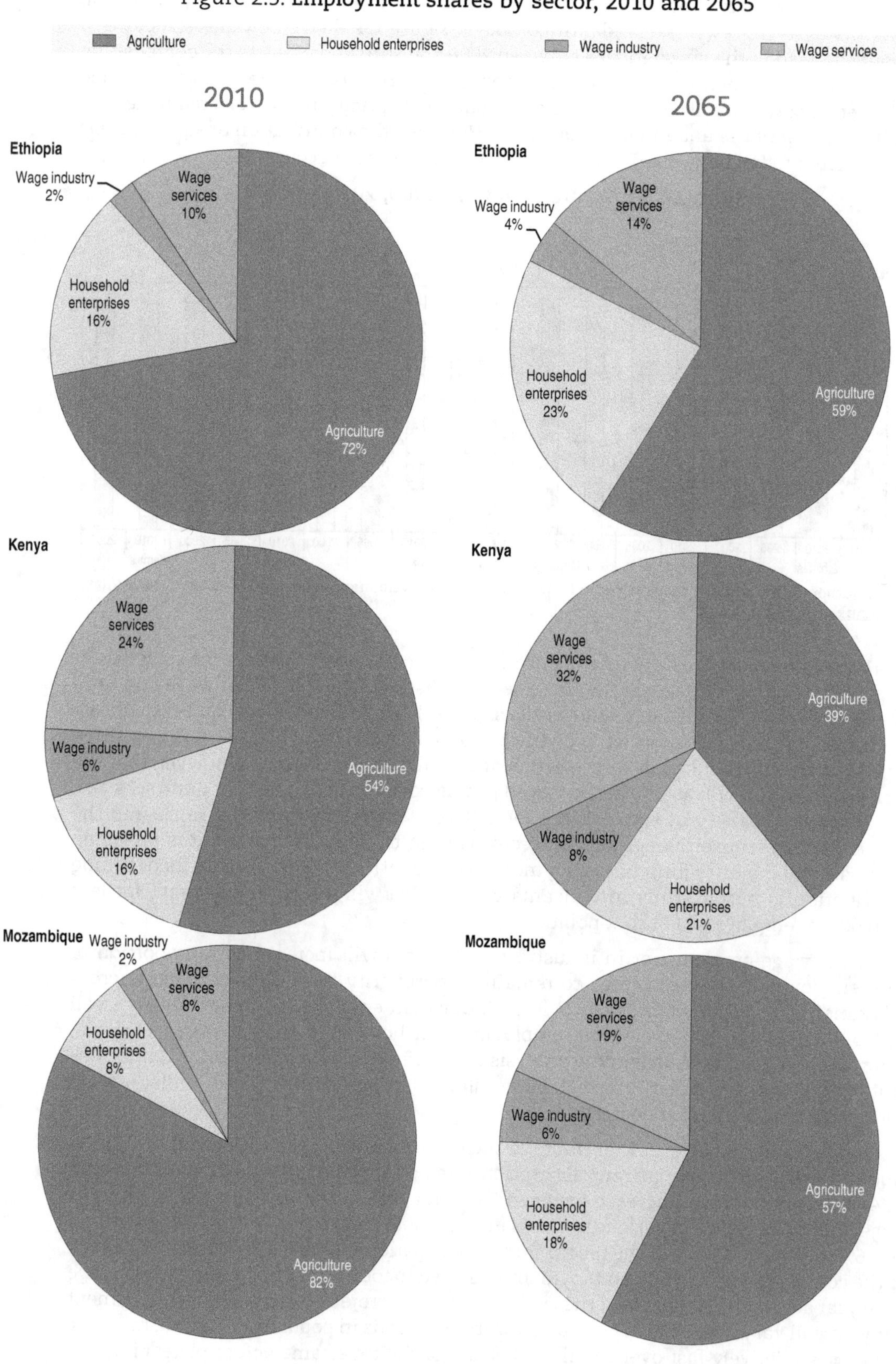

Figure 2.5 **Employment shares by sector, 2010 and 2065** (cont.)

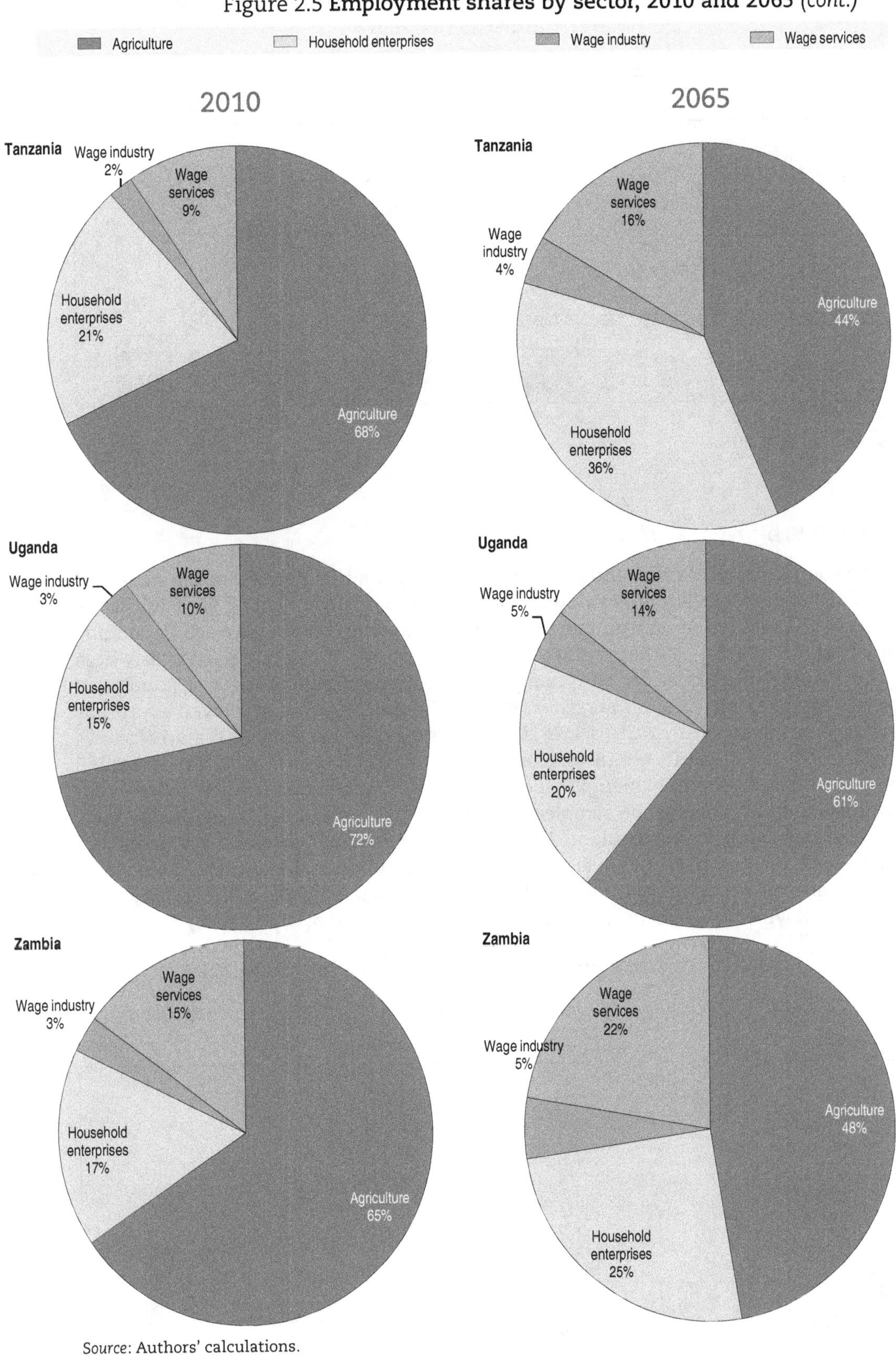

Source: Authors' calculations.

Figure 2.6. **Employment creation forecasts by sector 2015-2065,
agriculture as residual**

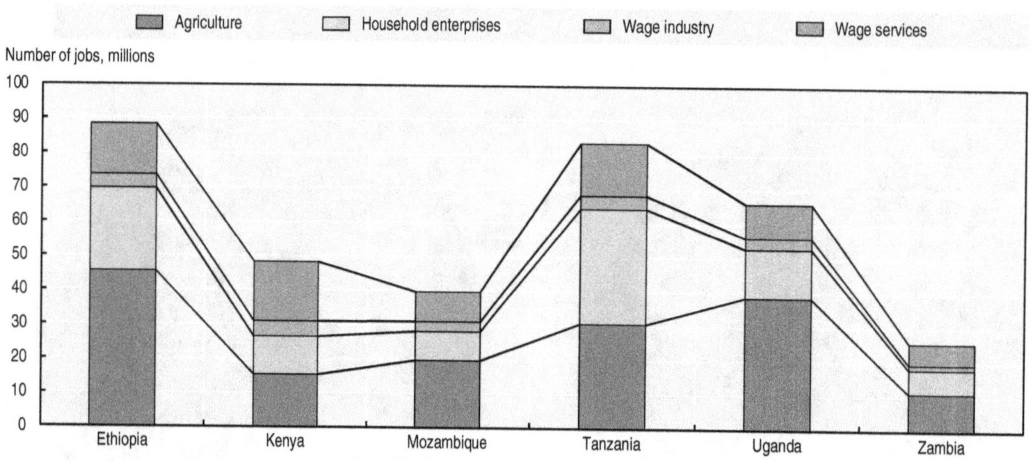

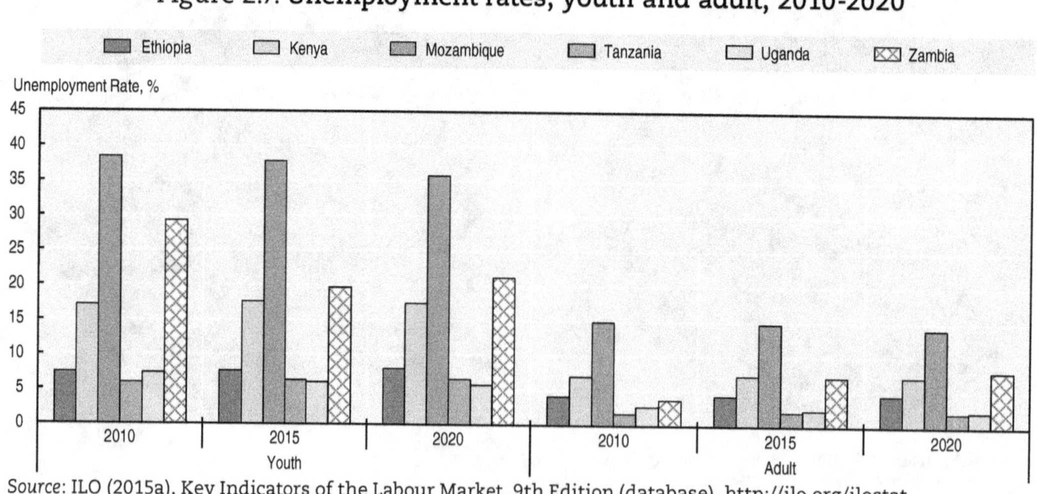

Source: Authors' calculations.

Ensuring the youth are not left behind

The youth cohorts of today and tomorrow are likely to suffer most from the combined effects of rapid population growth and slow structural change. Among each of the six countries, the rate of unemployment is higher than among the working age population as a whole: ILO (2015a) estimates and projections (Figure 2.7) indicate particularly high youth unemployment rates for Mozambique, Zambia and Kenya. If rates of population growth relative to job creation persist in Kenya, the number of unemployed youth has been projected to double by 2035 (UNDP, 2013). Table 2.2 (also based on ILO figures) shows a high proportion of youth not in employment, education or training in Tanzania and Zambia. For now, high youth unemployment rates appear to be compatible with low adult unemployment rates across the sample except in Mozambique, where the ILO also finds relatively high adult unemployment. However, exclusion from the labour market at a young age is likely to have an adverse impact on this cohort's labour-market outcomes further along the lifecycle: youth unemployment is associated with lower earnings and inferior employment prospects later in life (ILO, 2010; ILO, 2015b; OECD, 2010).

Figure 2.7. **Unemployment rates, youth and adult, 2010-2020**

Source: ILO (2015a), Key Indicators of the Labour Market, 9th Edition (database), http://ilo.org/ilostat.

Prolonging the length of time the youth spend in education will be of critical importance. Not only will this ease pressure on the labour market but it will also allow young people to develop the skills needed to find work and be productive. While net enrolment in primary school averaged 86% across the six sample countries across 2008 and 2012, net enrolment in secondary school averages just 30% (UNESCO, 2016).

Although higher educational attainment is often associated with improved employment prospects, the relationship does not always hold: in Ethiopia, Rwanda, Uganda and Tanzania, the unemployment rate is higher for those with secondary education or above than for those with basic or no education (UNESCO, 2013; UNECA, 2016), implying a mismatch between the skills young people acquire at school and the demands of the labour market (Kew, 2015). This is a worrying phenomenon: if continuing education past primary school fails to generate clear returns then many households will be unwilling to bear the costs of sending a child to school rather than putting them to work.

Table 2.2. **Youth not in employment, education or training (NEETs)[2]**

	Year	Age range	Per cent
Mozambique	2012	15-24	10.1
Tanzania	2012	15-24	31.8
Uganda	2013	15-24	5.9
Zambia	2012	15-29	28.3

Source: ILO (2015a), Key Indicators of the Labour Market, 9th Edition (database), http://ilo.org/ilostat.

Governments need to unlock the potential of youth entrepreneurship rather than rely on the formal sector to create jobs. In a context where the formal sector absorbs only a small proportion of new labour market entrants, many young people already find themselves in own-account work in the informal sector. This phenomenon is likely to increase as more young people enter the labour market. Making self-employment more profitable is likely to be the most important route out of poverty for millions of young people; doing so requires a co-ordinated response that tackles a number of the challenges to youth entrepreneurship, including how to foster the appropriate skills and improve access to capital.

Sexual and reproductive health (SRH) services can generate a number of very important benefits for the youth: they can address the unmet need for contraception (discussed in Chapter 1), reduce teenage pregnancy and prevent the spread of HIV/AIDS and other infections. Across Africa, however, provision of SRH services is failing to meet the needs of young people (Prata, Weidert and Sreenivas, 2013). SRH needs not only to be scaled up dramatically but should also be specifically tailored to young people (for example, by emphasising privacy and confidentiality) and particularly to adolescent women, who are often at greater risk of stigmatisation than adolescent men (Tylee et al., 2007).

Given the higher prevalence of HIV/AIDS in urban areas, expanding SRH services in cities – and particularly in informal settlements – will be very important (Renzaho et al., 2017). The cost of meeting demand for SRH services for the youth will rise as this cohort continues to grow but this investment would not only improve human capital among young people but also help to reduce the total fertility rate.

Population growth and inequality make poverty eradication a long-term challenge

Projecting the rate of economic growth across the six economies provides a framework for analysing future poverty dynamics. The first step is to identify how aggregate income gains will be distributed on the basis of the Gini coefficient. Figure 2.8, which sets out observations of the Gini coefficients by country between 1989 and 2012, shows significant variation between the six countries. Inequality has been consistently highest in Zambia and lowest in Ethiopia over this period, with a difference of more than 20% between these two according to the most recent data. The relatively rapid economic growth experienced over this period has not been associated with significant changes to the distribution of income in the majority of countries though there was a notable increase in Ethiopia. The poverty projections presented in this section assume that inequality will stay at its current level between 2015 and 2065, in accordance with a recent IMF finding that inequality appears to have remained broadly unchanged overall in sub-Saharan Africa, although there is variation across countries (IMF, 2015).

Figure 2.8. **Gini coefficients, 1989 to 2012**

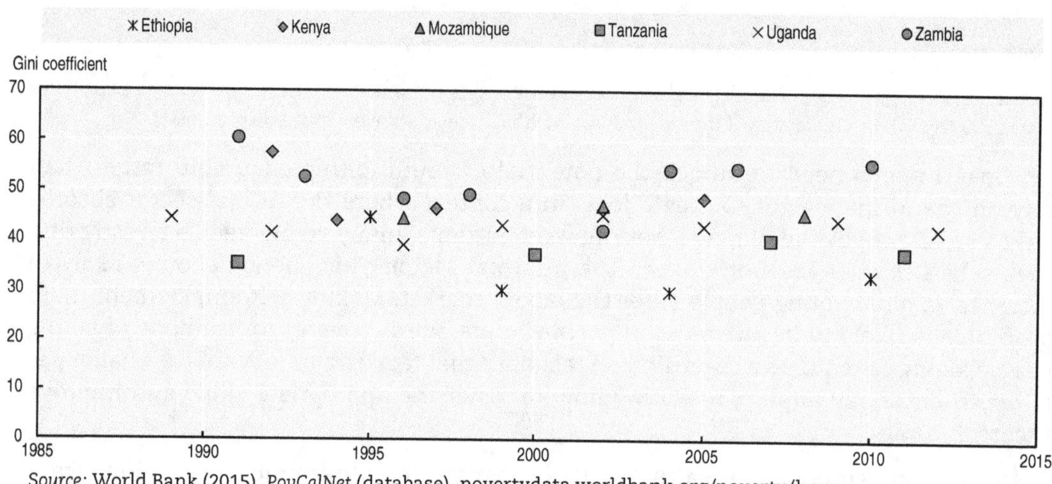

Source: World Bank (2015), *PovCalNet* (database), <u>povertydata.worldbank.org/poverty/home</u>.

The current level of poverty, the size of the poverty gap and the level of inequality across the sample countries in 2015 are shown in Table 2.3. These are extrapolations of historic trends.[3] As with the rates of inequality, the headcount poverty ratio and the poverty gap vary across the sample. Mozambique's poverty rate and poverty gap are highest among the sample, indicating that it will have the furthest to go in terms of eliminating poverty, while the headcount ratio and poverty gap are lowest in Kenya. However, Kenya also has the second-highest level of inequality, which will dampen the poverty-reducing effect of its per capita income gains over the sample period. Zambia has the second-highest headcount poverty ratio, the second-largest income gap and (by some distance) the highest level of inequality.

None of the six countries are likely to achieve the first Sustainable Development Goal – to eradicate poverty – by 2030 or for many years after. Figure 2.9 shows projected poverty headcounts against the World Bank's two updated poverty thresholds: USD 1.90 per day (extreme poverty) and USD 3.10 per day.[4] On a 20-year view, poverty headcount ratios against the USD 1.90 benchmark (left-hand panel) will range from 9% to 35% in 2035. On a 50-year view, only three countries will have poverty headcount ratios of less than 5% against the USD 1.90 benchmark: Ethiopia, Tanzania and Uganda. Against the USD 3.10 benchmark, only Ethiopia is projected to reduce poverty to below 10% by 2065.

Table 2.3. **Gini coefficients, poverty headcounts and poverty gaps, 2015**
Consumption based poverty line, USD 1.90 per person per day, 2011 PPP

	Gini coefficient	Headcount ratio	Poverty gap
Ethiopia	33.2	25.5	8.3
Kenya	48.5	24.4	7.8
Mozambique	45.6	55.2	22.1
Tanzania	37.8	26.7	8.8
Uganda	42.4	31.3	10.7
Zambia	55.6	47.7	18.3

Source: Authors' calculations based on World Bank (2015), World Development Indicators (database), http://data.worldbank.org/products/wdi.

Figure 2.9. **Headcount poverty ratios, USD 1.90 and 3.10 per day (2015-2065)**

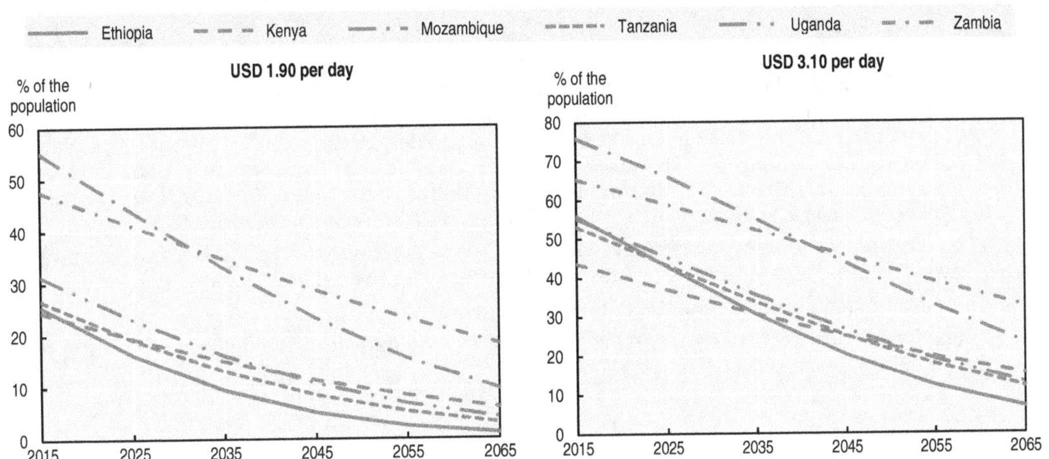

Source: World Bank (2015), *World Development Indicators* (database), http://data.worldbank.org/products/wdi.

At the current rate of progress, the number of extremely poor individuals across the six countries will decline only slightly between 2015 and 2035, from 86.3 million to 74 million, then drop to 39.4 million in 2065 (Figure 2.10). The decline in poverty in Ethiopia is responsible for much of this reduction: it is the only country where the absolute number of poor is projected to decline throughout the timeframe according to both poverty lines. In Kenya, Tanzania and Uganda, the number of extremely poor individuals will decline only slowly over the 50 years, while the number of poor as defined by the USD 3.10 threshold will increase between 2015 and 2035 before returning to its initial level. In Mozambique, poverty as defined by both lines initially increases before declining towards the end of the timeframe, while in Zambia the absolute number of poor individuals is projected to grow throughout the survey period against both measures.

Figure 2.10. **Number of poor, USD 1.90 and 3.10 per day (2015-2065)**

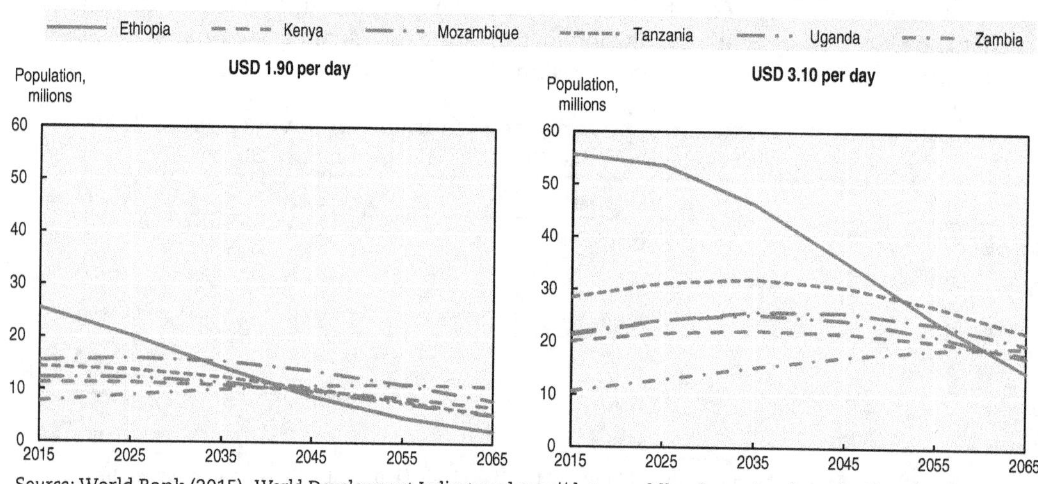

Source: World Bank (2015), *World Development Indicators*, http://data.worldbank.org/products/wdi.

Notes

1. National accounts data require a certain degree of caution. Analysing the performance of 44 countries against 71 indicators, the African Development Bank came to the conclusion that five of the six countries in this study performed adequately on 60%-70% of the indicators (Ethiopia the best, followed by Mozambique, Kenya, Zambia and Tanzania), with Uganda lagging at just under 50% (African Development Bank, Statistics Department, *Situational Analysis of the Reliability of Economic Statistics in Africa: Special Focus on GDP measurement,* June 2013).

2. The ILO does not provide an estimate for youth not in employment, education and training in Kenya. The Ethiopian estimate includes children between the ages of 10 and 14.

3. The methodology for updating the data is described in Annex 2.A2.

4. These figures are derived by updating the latest survey data for each country according to a methodology described in Annex 2.A2.

References

African Development Bank (2013), *Situational Analysis of the Reliability of Economic Statistics in Africa: Special Focus on GDP measurement*, AfDB Statistics Department, Abidjan.

AfDB, OECD and UNDP (2015), *African Economic Outlook 2015: Regional Development and Spatial Inclusion*, OECD Publishing, Paris, http://dx.doi.org/10.1787/aeo-2015-en.

de Vries, G., K. de Vries and M. Timmer (2013), "Structural Transformation in Africa: Static Gains, Dynamic Losses", *Journal of Development Studies*, Vol. 51, Issue 6, pp. 674-688.

Easterly, W. et al. (1993), "Good policy or good luck? Country growth performance and temporary shocks", *Journal of Monetary Economics*, 32(3): 459–483.

Foster, V. and Briceño-Garmendia, C. (2010), *Africa's infrastructure: a time for transformation*, World Bank, Washington, DC, https://openknowledge.worldbank.org/handle/10986/2692.

Fox, L. et al. (2013), "Africa's got work to do: Employment prospects in the new century", *IMF Working Paper* WP/13/201, International Monetary Fund, Washington, DC.

ILO (2015a), *Key Indicators of the Labour Market, 9th edition* (database), http://ilo.org/ilostat, (accessed June 2016).

ILO (2015b), *Global Employment Trends for Youth 2015: Scaling up investments in decent jobs for youth*, International Labour Organisation, Geneva.

ILO (2010), *Global Employment Trends for Youth, August 2010: Special issue on the impact of the global economic crisis on youth*, International Labour Organization, Geneva.

IMF (2016), *World Economic Outlook* (database), April, imf.org/en/data (accessed June 2016).

IMF (2015), *World Economic Outlook* (database), October, imf.org/en/data (accessed January 2016).

IMF (2015), *Regional Economic Outlook, Sub-Saharan Africa: Dealing with the Gathering Clouds*, World Economic and Financial Surveys, International Monetary Fund, Washington, DC.

Kew, J. (2015), "Africa's Young Entrepreneurs Unlocking the potential for a brighter future", International Development Research Centre [IDRC], Cape Town.

McKinsey Global Institute (2015), *Global growth: Can Productivity Save the Day in an Aging World?*, McKinsey & Company, McKinsey Global Institute.

McMillan, M., D. Rodrik and Í. Verduzco-Gallo (2014), "Globalization, Structural Change, and Productivity Growth, with an Update on Africa," *World Development* 63, pp. 11-32.

McMillan, M. and K. Harttgen (2014), "What is driving the 'African growth miracle?", *African Development Bank Group Working Paper* No. 209, African Development Bank, Tunis.

OECD (2016), *GDP long-term forecast* (indicator), accessed January 2016, http://dx.doi.org/10.1787/d927bc18-en.

OECD (2010), *Education at a Glance 2010 – OECD Indicators*, OECD Publishing, Paris. http://dx.doi.org/10.1787/eag-2010-en.

Page, J. (2013), "Should Africa Industrialize?", in A. Szirmai, W. Naude and L. Alcorta (eds.), *Pathways to Industrialization in the Twenty-First Century: New Challenges and Emerging Paradigms*, Oxford University Press, Oxford.

Prata, N., K. Weidert and A. Sreenivas (2013), "Meeting the need: youth and family planning in sub-Saharan Africa", *Contraception* 88(1), pp. 83-90.

Renzaho, A.M.N. et al. (2017), "Sexual, Reproductive Health Needs, and Rights of Young People in Slum Areas of Kampala, Uganda: A Cross Sectional Study", *PLoS ONE* 12(1), pp. 1-21, http://dx.doi.org/10.1371/journal.pone.0169721.

Rodrik, D. (2015), "Premature Deindustrialization", *NBER Working Paper Series*, No. 20935, National Bureau for Economic Research, http://dx.doi.org/10.3386/w20935.

Rodrik, D. (2014), "An African growth miracle?", *NBER Working Paper Series*, No. 20188, National Bureau for Economic Research, http://dx.doi.org/10.3386/w20188.

Tylee, A. et al. (2007), "Youth-friendly primary-care services: how are we doing and what more needs to be done?", *The Lancet* 369(9572), pp. 1565-73, http://dx.doi.org/0.1016/S0140-6736(07)60371-7.

UN DESA (2015), *World Population Prospects: The 2015 Revision*, United Nations Department of Economic and Social Affairs, New York.

UNECA (2016), *Social cohesion in Eastern Africa*, United Nations Economic Commission for Africa, Subregional Office for East Africa, Addis Ababa, http://hdl.handle.net/10855/22957.

UNDP (2013), "Kenya's youth employment challenge", discussion paper, United Nations Development Programme, New York.

UNESCO (2016), *UIS.Stat* (database), data.uis.unesco.org, accessed October 2016.

UNESCO (2013), "Educational Attainment and employment outcomes", Background paper prepared for the Education for All Global Monitoring Report 2013/4, United Nations Economic Scientific and Cultural Organization, Paris.

World Bank (2016), *World Development Indicators* (database), accessed October 2016, http://data.worldbank.org/products/wdi.

World Bank (2015), *World Development Indicators* (database), accessed June 2015, http://data.worldbank.org/products/wdi.

World Bank (2015), *PovCalNet* (database), World Bank, Washington, DC, accessed December 2015, povertydata.worldbank.org/poverty/home.

UN DESA (2014), *World Urbanization Prospects: The 2014 Revision*, United Nations Department of Economic and Social Affairs, United Nations, New York.

Annex 2.A1. Sensitivity analysis for employment projections

There are a number of factors that could enhance the level of formal employment over the projected timeframe, including:

- A more rapid demographic transition, leading to slower population growth;
- Higher long-term growth in per capita income;
- A greater shift towards industrial and services output;
- Higher elasticity of wage employment in industry and services with respect to the growth of output.

To carry out a sensitivity analysis, four scenarios are successively built up as follows:

1. Population develops in accordance with the "Lower 80" rather than the "Median" United Nations probabilistic projection, under which East Africa's TFR has fallen to replacement rate by 2065 (as shown in Figure 2.A1.1).

2. Scenario A plus a 20% increase in the long-term growth rate, which is driven by a higher productivity assumption.

3. Scenario B plus a 5% increase in the share of industry and services by 2065.

4. Scenario C plus a 10% increase in the employment growth to sectoral output growth elasticities for wage industry and wage service employment.

Figure 2.A1.1. **Median versus lower 80 population projections for East Africa: Population size and total fertility rate (right-hand side)**

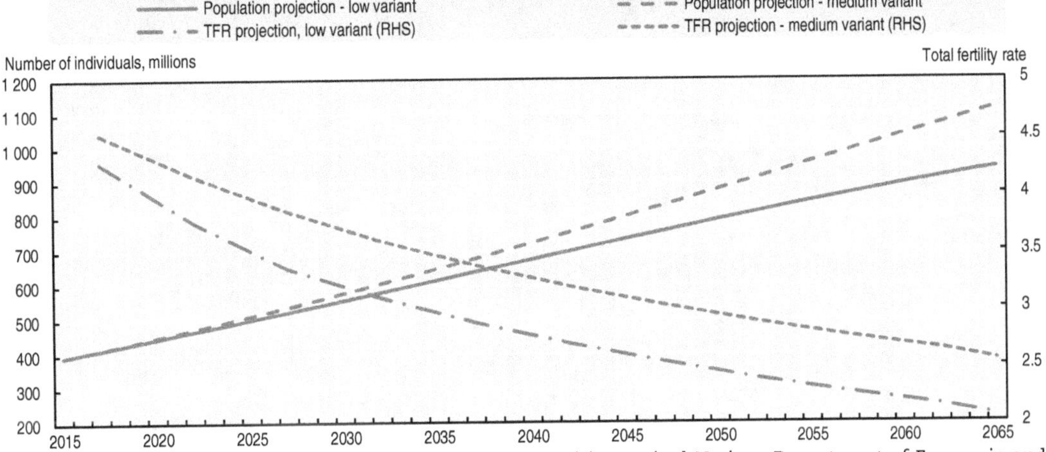

Source: UN DESA (2015), *World Population Prospects, 2015 Revision*, United Nations Department of Economic and Social Affairs, United Nations, New York.

The table below sets out the proportion of wage employment in total employment in 2065 in the base case and in the four alternative scenarios. Even with the successive changes in factors favouring the growth of wage employment, the conclusion reached from the baseline projection continues to hold, except in Kenya under Scenarios B, C and D. It should be borne in mind that the probability of each scenario materialising drops progressively. No corresponding downside set of scenarios has been created, since they would all strengthen the conclusion drawn from the baseline projection.

Table 2.A1.1. Share of wage employment in total employment in 2065

	Ethiopia (%)	Kenya (%)	Mozambique (%)	Tanzania (%)	Uganda (%)	Zambia (%)
Base case	17.4	38.5	24.0	19.5	18.6	25.1
Scenario A	21.4	46.1	29.1	23.8	22.5	31.2
Scenario B	26.0	56.0	35.3	29.0	27.4	37.9
Scenario C	27.3	58.8	37.1	30.4	28.7	39.8
Scenario D	30.7	66.5	45.2	36.4	33.5	47.2

Source: UN DESA (2015), *World Population Prospects: The 2015 Revision*, United Nations Department of Economic and Social Affairs, United Nations, New York.

Annex 2.A2. Basis for adjusting the headcount and poverty gap measures and updating them to 2015

The mathematical framework for adjusting headcount and poverty gap measures is the log-normal distribution. Income and consumption distributions are approximated by this distribution, which depends on two parameters, μ and σ. Once these are known, the entire distribution is specified. Two relationships are important. The Gini coefficient is given by:

$$Gini = 2\Phi(\sigma/\sqrt{2}) - 1, \qquad \text{(Equation 1)}$$

where $\Phi(.)$ is the cumulative normal distribution function, and the mean of the distribution is

$$m = exp(\mu + \sigma^2/2), \qquad \text{(Equation 2)}$$

The Gini coefficient is assumed constant throughout. This enables one to calculate for each country, using Equation 1. Then the mean of the distribution (monthly per capita income in 2011 purchasing power parity US dollars) can be used in Equation 2 to find μ.

Denote any level of monthly income per capita in 2011 PPP US dollars by y. If y is log-normally distributed, then $ln(y)$ is normally distributed, and a z-value can be calculated in order to refer to the standard normal distribution, with a mean of zero and a standard deviation of 1. Thus

$$z = (ln(y) - \mu)/\sigma, \qquad \text{(Equation 3)}$$

and, in particular, when y is the poverty line p (USD 57.8 per month)

$$z_p = (ln(p) - \mu)/\sigma, \qquad \text{(Equation 4)}$$

The headcount measure of poverty then becomes

$$H = \Phi(z_p) \qquad \text{(Equation 5)}$$

The poverty gap measure can be calculated from the conditional expectation of y up to the threshold p, $E[y|y < p]$. This conditional expectation yields the mean income of people below the poverty line, from which the poverty gap can be readily calculated.

The method also allows one to update the headcount and poverty measures. If σ is constant and mean income per capita is growing at rate g per annum, and we update at intervals of t (say ten years), then the median grows at the same rate as the mean. Now the median of the log normal distribution is $exp(\mu)$, so $\mu = ln(y^*)$, so, where y^* is the median income. Denote the median income in a base year as $y^*(0)$, and the median income after t years as $y^*(t)$. Then

$$y^*(t) = y^*(0) \cdot (1 + g)^t, \text{ so taking logarithms}$$
$$\mu(t) = \mu(0) + t \cdot ln(1 + g) \qquad \text{(Equation 6)}$$

so that Equation (4) becomes

$$z_p(t) = (ln(p) - \mu(t))/\sigma,$$

and the calculation of the headcount and poverty gap proceed as before.

Equation 6 holds only when the Gini coefficient, and hence σ, remains constant over time. In this case, the median income and the mean income grow at the same rate.

To generalise it to the case where inequality varies over time, the mean income $m(t)$ reflects the growth rate g so that

$ln(m(t)) = ln(m(0)) + t \cdot ln(1+g)m$ so that, from Equation 2,

$\mu(t) + \sigma^2(t)/2 = \mu(0) + \sigma^2(0)/2 = t \cdot ln(1+g)$, or

$$\mu(t) = \mu(0) + t \cdot ln(1+g) - (\sigma^2(t) - \sigma^2(0))/2 \qquad \text{(Equation 7)}$$

Compared with Equation (6), Equation (7) has an additional term on the right hand side, which accounts for changes in inequality.

It remains to adjust the headcount and poverty gap for the three countries in which the survey estimate of consumption per head is significantly different from the national accounts estimate of consumption per head, and to update all estimates to 2015. For the three countries, the headcount ratio was taken as the mean of the survey-based estimate and the national accounts based estimate in 2011 PPP US dollars. Then the method of updating the estimates to 2015 outlined above was applied.

Chapter 3

Towards a long-term perspective on social protection

The previous chapters identified key emerging demographic, economic and environmental trends that will affect livelihoods in East Africa over the next 50 years. This chapter will demonstrate how social protection can help countries in the region adapt to these coming challenges at the same time as it supports the current efforts of governments to eradicate poverty, reduce vulnerability and promote the sustainable, inclusive and people-centred development envisaged by Agenda 2063. This chapter identifies ways in which the previous findings can be turned into policy directions that could foster the development of social protection systems able to address the many challenges that lie ahead. These policy directions are grouped into seven fundamental challenges for social protection planners.

Seven grand challenges for social protection

The previous chapters present a number of emerging demographic, economic and environmental trends that will constrain development, threaten human well-being, and jeopardise the region's progress in eradicating poverty as well as its vision for social protection. Based on the findings of the previous two chapters, this chapter identifies seven grand challenges that confront governments in the six sample countries. In each case, social protection should be an integral part of the policy response. The challenges are as follows:

- Solve the last mile problem of reaching the extreme poor. In a context where population growth and inequality will act as brakes on poverty reduction, social assistance will be an essential means of accelerating the decline in poverty across the six countries. However, its impact is currently constrained by low coverage and poor targeting: as Agenda 2063 notes, social protection programmes in Africa currently cover less than 20% of the poorest quintile.

- Promote social insurance in a context of high informality. Social insurance arrangements enable individuals to protect themselves against the risk of falling into poverty. However, coverage is very low across Africa because most existing arrangements exclude informal and rural workers.

- Confront the employment challenge. A boom in the working-age population has the potential to transform the continent, but only if new entrants to the labour market can find productive employment.

- Adapt to rapid urbanisation. Coverage of social assistance programmes is lower in cities than in rural areas. With East Africa's cities set to continue their rapid growth over the next 50 years, urban poverty is set to increase and social protection needs to adapt to meet the challenge.

- Adapting to climate change and mitigating its effect. The effects of climate change are often felt most keenly by the poor and vulnerable; social protection can support these groups not only to recover from climate shocks but also to adapt to climate change and protect their homes and livelihoods.

- Harness a demographic dividend. Policies to accelerate the fertility decline and enhance productivity are essential if Africa is to harness the potential of its favourable demographic conditions.

- Increase financing for social protection. Agenda 2063 calls for spending on social protection to more than double. While this is essential for establishing sustainable social protection systems, it is important to avoid hurting the poor when exploring ways to generate these revenues.

The challenges outlined above are complex and interlinked. They also have different timeframes and require social protection policy makers to create solutions in collaboration with institutions outside the social sector. It is essential that social protection policy makers start considering the appropriate responses to these challenges today: social protection systems are in their infancy across the six countries and should be designed not only with current challenges in mind but also in such a way as to protect individuals and economies to the risks that lie ahead. Adopting a long-term perspective is also an important means of managing the trade-offs between the different challenges, given that the six countries will lack the resources to address them simultaneously.

The policy response to each of these challenges will require a combination of social assistance, social insurance and labour market policies. This combination is unlikely to be effective without a significant degree of integration between these pillars at an administrative, operational and institutional level. At the administrative level, different social protection schemes can share data and monitoring systems; at the operational level, social protection schemes often share enrolment and delivery systems; and at the policy level, a single institution might be required to co-ordinate social protection activities across sectors and ministries. At the same time, social protection is increasingly shown to generate positive economic externalities; it is therefore important to link social protection systems to broader economic strategies to facilitate its role in promoting inclusive and pro-poor growth (European Commission, 2015).

Box 3.1. **Defining social protection**

Social protection is subject to numerous different definitions which vary not only between individual countries but also between international organisations. The International Labour Organization defines social protection as "[t]he set of public measures that a society provides for its members to protect them against economic and social distress that would be caused by the absence or a substantial reduction of income from work as a result of various contingencies (sickness, maternity, employment injury, unemployment, invalidity, old age, and death of the breadwinner); the provision of health care; and the provision of benefits for families with children."

Yet even this wide-ranging definition is not appropriate for every country; as the ILO acknowledges, "Differing cultures, values, traditions and institutional and political structures affect definitions of social protection as well as the choice of how protection should be provided" (Bonilla Garcia and Gruat, 2003). In the social protection strategies of the six countries studied here, the term is defined as follows:

- Ethiopia: A set of formal and informal interventions that aim to reduce social and economic risks, vulnerabilities and deprivations for all people and to facilitate equitable growth.

- Kenya: Policies and actions, including legislative measures, that enhance the capacity of and opportunities for the poor and vulnerable to improve and sustain their lives, livelihoods and welfare, enable income-earners and their dependents to maintain a reasonable level of income through decent work, and ensure access to affordable healthcare, social security, and social assistance (Republic of Kenya, 2011).

- Mozambique's social protection law identifies three pillars: basic social security for citizens with no means (covering social transfers, health, education and economic inclusion), obligatory social security and complementary social security.

- Tanzania: Social protection describes traditional family and community support structures, and interventions by state and non-state actors that support individuals, households and communities to prevent, manage, and overcome the risks threatening their present and future security and well-being, and to embrace opportunities for their development and for social and economic progress.

- Uganda: Social protection refers to public and private interventions to address risks and vulnerabilities that expose individuals to income insecurity and social deprivation, leading to undignified lives (Republic of Uganda, 2015).

- Zambia: Social protection is a poverty-reduction strategy that promotes human development, social equity and human rights through policies and programmes that seek to promote the livelihoods and welfare of the poorest and those most vulnerable to risks and shocks.

Meeting the challenges identified in this report will require not only greater financial resources to be allocated to social protection but will also require significant enhancement of countries' capacity to design, deliver, monitor and adapt social protection policies and programmes. Establishing a long-term strategy specifically for capacity development both at the individual and institutional level, for every sphere of government and among the broader social protection community should be a core focus of social protection planning.

The policies proposed in this chapter are of major importance to all aspects of society, not just the governments that might implement them. Involving social partners – not only organised labour and business but also civil society organisations – in reform processes is an essential means of ensuring that the interests of different components of society are heard, thereby promoting policy-making that is balanced and appropriate to the needs of the whole population (European Commission, 2016). Not only is this likely to lead to better policies but it is also important in terms of securing public support for reforms. Moreover, in a context where governments might lack the capacity to enforce policies, social partners can be a crucial ally in securing participation or compliance among their respective constituencies.

Solving the last mile problem of eliminating extreme poverty

Africa's poverty rate has declined in the past 20 years but remains above 40%. At the current rate of progress, economic growth alone will take generations to reduce headcount poverty across the six countries; due to rapid population growth, the absolute number of poor households will show little decline and might even increase in some countries. Inequality acts as a brake on poverty reduction.

Agenda 2063 and SDG #1 both target the eradication of poverty yet the results of Chapter 2 indicate this is unlikely to occur for a long time. Accelerating the decline will require governments to find a solution to the last-mile problem: the challenge of reaching the extreme and chronic poor. These are the individuals and households who are not benefitting from growth in the broader economy because they are structurally excluded (for reasons of age, disability, place of residence or many other factors) from the major drivers of poverty reduction. Social assistance is the most feasible means of reaching these groups[1] but in the six sample countries such programmes are undermined by difficulties in targeting transfers.

Targeting errors fall into two categories: errors of exclusion (individuals whom the government considers to be in greatest need of transfers do not receive them) and errors of inclusion (individuals whose need for such programmes is not so great do receive transfers). The World Bank's ASPIRE database indicates the scale of the exclusion problem: according to the latest available data (shown in Table 3.1), coverage of social assistance in the six countries among the poorest quintile ranged from just 1% (Zambia in 2010) to 76% (Uganda in 2012). Table 3.1 and Figure 3.1 also reveal the level of inclusion errors in Kenya, Tanzania and Uganda. The proportion of total social assistance beneficiaries who were in the poorest quintile in Kenya and Tanzania was below 20%, while in all three countries the richest quintile captured more than half the benefits of social assistance.

At the same time, the ASPIRE database indicates that the level of spending is – in theory – less of a problem. Assuming perfect targeting, the level of expenditure on social assistance across the respective countries is sufficient to eradicate extreme poverty.[2] Moreover, if all benefits accruing to the top quintile had been reallocated to the poor, it would have been possible not only to grant benefits to all the poor but also to increase the average benefit size among the poor.

In practice, however, global experience indicates that perfect targeting is not possible.[3] While this phenomenon is often linked to imperfect design and implementation of social assistance programmes, it is also caused by imperfect information. It is often very difficult to understand who the poorest individuals are, how poor they are and where they reside. It is important that countries and development partners invest resources in improving statistical information (as is discussed later in this chapter) and administrative capacity.

However, there are limits to how effective this can be. Attempts to reduce inclusion errors typically increase the level of exclusion errors while efforts to reduce exclusion errors increase inclusion errors (Coady, Grosh and Hoddinott, 2004).

Table 3.1. **Indicators of social assistance performance**

Country	Year	Coverage	Beneficiary incidence
		Quintile 1 (%)	Quintile 1 (%)
Ethiopia	2010	16.2	-
Kenya	2005	34.4	13.4
Mozambique	2008	7.7	-
Tanzania	2010	13.4	16.5
Uganda	2012	76.1	42.3
Zambia	2010	1.0	-

Note: Coverage denotes the percentage of a given group that receives social assistance, while beneficiary incidence indicates how social assistance beneficiaries are distributed across income groups.
Source: World Bank (2017), ASPIRE (database).

Due to the many challenges associated with means-testing benefits in low- and lower-middle income countries, poverty-reduction programmes increasingly rely on a range of proxy variables (such as household size or housing) as a means of identifying households in greatest need. This information is then inserted into a statistical model which weights the information and computes eligibility. Brown, Ravallion and van de Walle (2016) compare the theoretical performance of a widely-used proxy means test (PMT) against a universal basic income (UBI) in nine African countries, including Ethiopia, Tanzania and Uganda. They find that, given a social assistance budget equivalent to the poverty gap, the PMT performs only slightly better than the UBI in reducing poverty. Moreover, the complexity of the PMT methodology means that the targeting process for a given programme might lack transparency, which can be a source of discontent at a local level and undermine a programme's legitimacy (Kidd, Gelders and Bailey-Athias, 2017).

There is also an important political economy aspect to the debate around targeting. Devoting a significant amount of government resources to a programme which only benefits the poorest members of society is challenging, since they typically lack a political constituency. Moreover, such schemes risk being perceived as ill-deserved hand-outs that will encourage dependency and disincentivise participation in the labour force. On the other hand, the middle class might be more in favour of such programmes if they benefit from them as well.

In order to accelerate the decline in poverty, spending on social assistance across the six countries will need to increase irrespective of targeting errors. Improving the information base and administrative capacity of social assistance programmes will take time and money but is an important means of maximising the impact of spending of such interventions. Nonetheless, these efforts cannot hope to eliminate targeting errors completely. In order to eliminate extreme poverty the primary focus must be on reducing errors of exclusion even at the cost of increasing errors of inclusion in the short term. While this has major implications for the cost of such programmes, the combined longer-term effect of higher expenditure and reduced errors of exclusion would be a reduction in inequality, an effect which would be magnified if these transfers are increasingly financed through progressive domestic taxation.

Figure 3.1. Incidence of social assistance benefits across the sample countries

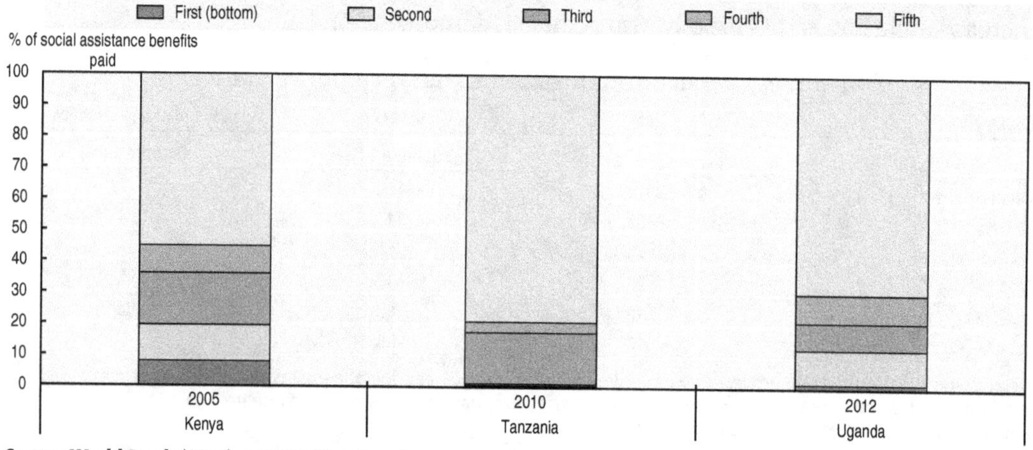

Source: World Bank (2017), ASPIRE (database).

Box 3.2. Current social assistance spending

It is not possible to quantify the current level of social protection spending across the six countries on a comparable basis. Annex 3.A2 provides a methodology for doing so, which incorporates data from a variety of sources, including the World Bank's ASPIRE database. Figure 3.2 shows the level of spending on social assistance across the sample countries for different years according to the ASPIRE database.

There are major problems with this information, stemming from poor data on the functional classification of government expenditure in the six countries and variable methods for imputation even within some of the same sources at different points in time. There is also the obvious point that the data is in some cases very out of date: spending in Tanzania has increased with the expansion of TASAF since 2009, while expenditure on the PSNP alone accounts for 1.2% of GDP (del Ninno, Coll-Black and Fallavier, 2015), which means that the figure for Ethiopia is also understated.

Figure 3.2. Social assistance spending across the sample countries

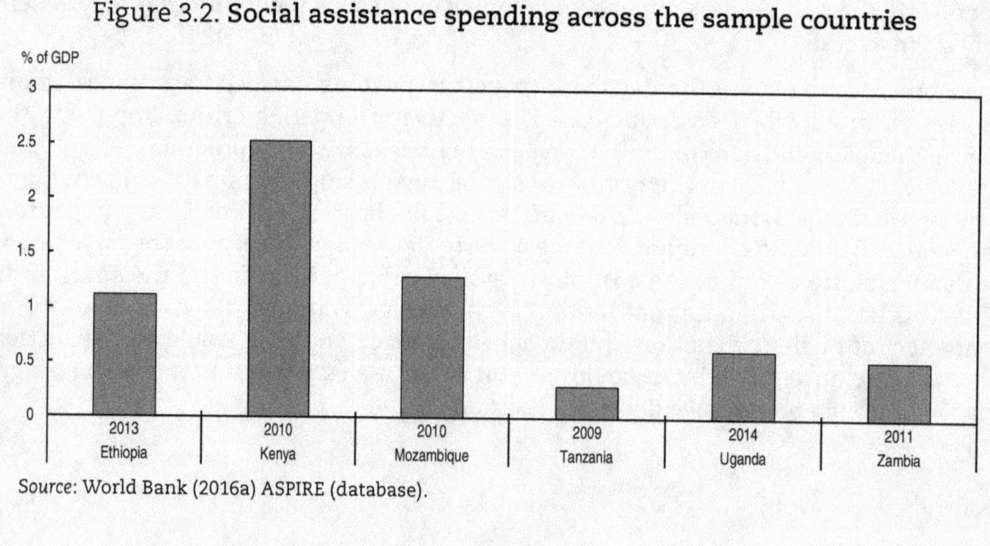

Source: World Bank (2016a) ASPIRE (database).

> **Box 3.2. Current social assistance spending** (*cont.*)
>
> By comparison, South Africa spent some 3.1% of GDP on its social grants system in 2016/17 (Republic of South Africa, 2017), which accounts for the bulk of its social protection spending and covers 17.0 million people, just under a third of the population. Brazil's flagship Bolsa Familia programme costs 0.5% of GDP but spending on non-contributory rural pensions accounts for 2.0% of GDP, while expenditure on contributory pensions accounted for 11.3% of GDP in 2015 (Cuevas and Karpowicz, 2016).

Social insurance holds the key to sustainable declines in poverty. Poverty and vulnerability are dynamic: the determinants will change over time and shocks can strike different groups in different places at different moments. Beegle et al. (2016) show that in many African countries transient poverty is higher than chronic poverty and there is significant clustering of poor and non-poor around the poverty line. This underscores the need to promote social insurance programmes among the non-poor as a means of promoting sustainable declines in poverty. Such arrangements provide an alternative source of income to beneficiaries that materialises automatically in response to an income shock, thereby preventing them from falling into poverty and relying on social assistance. The value of these mechanisms extends beyond the individual level: social insurance programmes automatically mitigate the impact of economic downturns by supporting aggregate demand. In the wake of the global financial crisis, public social spending across OECD countries increased from 19% of GDP in 2007 to an average of 22% of GDP over the period 2009-2012 despite significant budget pressures over this timeframe (OECD, 2012).

Enhancing social insurance coverage in a context of high informality

At the current rate of structural change, the overwhelming majority of the workforce across the six countries will remain in agricultural and informal employment, even 50 years from now. Moreover, the relative size of the elderly population will start to increase rapidly around 2040. Extremely low coverage of social insurance means that today's workforce is at risk of falling into poverty when they retire, if not before.

The population projections in Chapter 1 reveal that, while the elderly population was relatively small in 2015, it will experience rapid growth from around 2030 onwards across the sample countries. Higher life expectancy over the next 50 years will compound this growth: life expectancy at age 60 is expected to grow across the sample countries from an average of 17 years today to about 20 years in 2065. By expanding contributory rather than non-contributory pension arrangements, governments are released from the expense associated with supporting consumption among the elderly population. The sooner this is done, the better: workers need to contribute to social security arrangements for most of their careers in order to be sure of receiving an adequate income in old age.

The design and composition of social insurance arrangements, and particularly pension systems, varies across the six countries. However, they share the defining characteristic of very low coverage: only in Kenya is coverage estimated to exceed 10% of the working age population (Dorfman, 2015). Social protection strategies across the countries stress the need to increase coverage as fast as possible but they face a major challenge: their social insurance systems are mostly designed for individuals employed in the formal sector.

As Chapter 2 shows, the proportion of the workforce in formal employment is low today and is unlikely to increase significantly even over the long-term without a substantial acceleration in the rate of structural transformation. Informality will remain the norm. Only in Kenya is the proportion of the workforce in wage employment projected to exceed 30% over the next 50 years.

There are many reasons for the tendency to limit coverage to formal wage employment, including government's role in mandating, administering or regulating such arrangements and the administrative challenge inherent to contributions that might be irregular – either in terms of their size or the frequency with which they are made. It is also the case that many households do not have sufficient income to contribute at the rate required. Given that workers in the informal sector tend to be the most vulnerable, the result is a situation where those who most need the protection offered by social insurance are least able to access it.

Kenya's Mbao pension fund is showing the way forward. Since its establishment in 2009 as a voluntary private pension plan regulated by the Retirement Benefit Authority (RBA) for the informal sector, it has experienced rapid growth. In December 2014, the Mbao Pension scheme had 66 228 members and represented 46% of total members in Kenya's individual pension plans, though it remains relatively small in terms of assets (Retirement Benefits Authority, 2015). The Mbao Pension plan runs in parallel to the National Social Security Fund (NSSF) and has extended eligibility to any Kenyan nationals aged over 18 since 2014 in order to expand its coverage of the informal sector. The Mbao pension makes extensive use of mobile phone technology to facilitate transactions and is highly flexible in allowing for irregular and fluctuating contributions. As the government acknowledges, "[T]o effectively respond to the needs of informal sector workers, the NSSF will need to adopt flexible voluntary savings schemes similar to the Mbao Pension Plan" (Republic of Kenya and World Bank, 2012).

Labour organisations in the informal sector can be an important channel for promoting social insurance. The rapid growth in the informal workforce has been associated with a decline in trade union membership in recent decades (Bonner and Spooner, 2011). However, this does not mean that workers have ceased to organise; rather, they do so through a more diverse set of associations and other structures which might lack the same bargaining power or political influence as formal trade unions but which nonetheless have considerable influence within a given sector (ILO, 2002). As a result, organised labour remains a valuable mechanism for promoting enrolment in social insurance arrangements, both private and public.

In Indonesia, for example, government ministries, labour organisations, business and civil society are represented on the National Social Security Council, which is overseeing the implementation of a new social security system. BPJS Ketenagakerjaan, the government agency which provides cover for occupational accidents, retirement savings and life insurance, is working with civil society organisations and employer associations to expand coverage of social insurance among the informal sector (Suryahadi et al., 2014, van Klaveren, Gregory and Schulten, 2015).

Another potential avenue for promoting access to social insurance is through formal enterprises such as farming companies that contract with large numbers of informal workers or producers along their value chain. These enterprises can act as "contribution aggregators" by deducting contributions from the payments they make to individuals, which the enterprises will deposit in appropriate social security arrangements on behalf of the workers. The frequency and amount of these contributions would depend on an individual's capacity to contribute.

Aside from the administrative constraints on expanding coverage, overcoming the behavioural impediments to enrolment in social insurance schemes will require efforts to improve the overall effectiveness of the system. Convincing individuals to set aside a portion of their money in arrangements which might impose rules on the timing or frequency of withdrawals rather than rely on precautionary saving requires them to have confidence in the institution managing these contributions and, crucially, to see some additional value to this approach rather than an individualist strategy. A danger of mandating contributions in a context where individuals do not see the value of such arrangements (or cannot afford the prescribed contribution rates) is that it can incentivise people to engage in informal activities.

As the World Bank notes in its report on Pensions in Sub-Saharan Africa (Dorfman, 2015), and as the experience of social health insurance suggests (Box 3.3), subsidised or matching contributions from the government are likely to hold the key to unlocking individuals' willingness to save. Establishing an appropriate design for subsidised or matching contributions comes with important challenges, however. Governments will need to address equity concerns with the approach, since it entails a transfer from the government to a (large) group of people who are likely to have access to the labour market and are therefore less likely to be poor than individuals who are excluded. The experiences emerging from Latin America, which has taken a lead in promoting matching defined contribution (MDCs) (Durán-Valverde et al., 2013), are not (yet) convincing: Colombia, Mexico and Peru have all enacted MDCs but have failed to extend coverage beyond groups that were already contributing (Carranza, Melguizo and Tuesta, 2012).

Box 3.3. **How social health insurance expanded coverage**

Many sub-Saharan African countries have traditionally organised public health coverage through government funding of public providers and by establishing an entitlement to everyone to use these public providers' services free of charge or for a low fee. However, in many (if not all) sub-Saharan countries, low investment in the public health sector and mostly non-existent incentives for quality and responsiveness have limited the availability and quality of public health services. This has led many individuals, even those with limited resources, to turn to private providers (where the quality of care can vary dramatically), which is associated with persistent financial barriers to accessing care and high levels of out-of-pocket expenditure.

Social health insurance (SHI) mechanisms exist as a means of harnessing the benefits of high-quality provision of health services in a cost-effective manner. However, comprehensive benefit packages are often limited to formal sector workers, meaning they face the same coverage constraints as other social insurance arrangements. In response, a number of countries have established mechanisms to increase coverage through approaches which combine contributory and tax-funded elements – as have already been implemented in Europe in response to the additional burden that ageing populations are placing on SHI systems.

Box 3.3. **How social health insurance expanded coverage** *(cont.)*

Ghana, for example, has established a National Health Insurance (NHI) mechanism to form the basis of a universal health system. A fixed portion of VAT revenues is allocated to the NHI through the so-called National Health Insurance Levy, which accounts for about 70% of total NHI revenues. Social security taxes provide an additional 23% while premiums account for just 5% (Lagomarsino et al., 2012; Blanchet et al., 2012). The poor and vulnerable are exempted from paying contributions. While the NHI is still maturing, it has already demonstrated that it can integrate those who cannot directly contribute while at the same time creating cross-subsidies from the direct contributions paid by those with greater capacity to pay.

Gabon has implemented a similar reform with earmarked and non-earmarked public funding mixed with contributions in order to extend coverage (Humphreys, 2013). Rwanda has taken a similar path (with a more decentralised structure) while Kenya is also moving in this direction (Lagomarsino et al, 2012; Mulupi, Kirigia and Chuma, 2013). An additional benefit of establishing SHI-style mechanisms (even when these are predominantly funded from general taxation) is that these arrangements separate purchaser and provider functions and thus establish better incentives to providers through strategic purchasing, which is currently an important issue for health reform in Mexico, for example (OECD, 2016a).

Sources: Humphreys (2013), "Gabon gets everyone under one social health insurance roof,"; Lagomarsino et al. (2012), "Moving towards universal health coverage: health insurance reforms in nine developing countries in Africa and Asia"; Blanchet et al. (2012), "The Effect of Ghana's National Health Insurance Scheme on Health Care Utilisation"; Mulupi, Kirigia and Chuma (2013), "Community perceptions of health insurance and their preferred design features: implications for the design of universal health coverage reforms in Kenya,"; OECD (2016a), *OECD Reviews of Health Systems: Mexico 2016.*

There will be major limitations to building on existing pension arrangements in sub-Saharan Africa to expand coverage to the informal sector. At present, 32 countries in sub-Saharan Africa base their systems on defined benefit arrangements, where contributions are pooled and vesting (minimum contribution) periods usually apply; such arrangements are poorly suited to erratic contributions and early withdrawals that are likely to characterise a system that caters to the informal sector. Pre-funded individual savings accounts (otherwise known as defined contribution arrangements) are better able to provide this degree of flexibility.

However, for funded accounts to be viable at scale, capital markets across the region will need to develop in order to provide an appropriate range of investment instruments and generate returns on these savings. For the most part, the capital markets of sub-Saharan Africa are very poorly developed: South Africa accounted for 77% of the USD 1 trillion combined market capitalisation of African exchanges at the end of 2015. Funded savings accounts also require a regulatory framework for the financial sector that promotes transparent and cost-effective management of these accounts, to prevent high costs and to protect contributors against investment risks. Even in these circumstances, however, individuals bear the risk of poor market returns.

Defined contribution arrangements are also reliant on a functioning annuities market to provide an adequate income in retirement. Sub-Saharan Africa's annuities market is poorly developed, in part because of the preponderance of national defined benefit arrangements (which pay a pension to contributors at retirement) and in part because a large proportion of employer funds pay contributors a once-off lump sum at retirement. If there is to be a large increase in coverage of funded individual accounts in the future, it must be accompanied by an expansion of the annuities market. Where such arrangements exist in Africa, they are most often used by wealthier individuals who have a sufficient accumulation of savings to provide a substantial monthly benefit. There is little incentive for low-income groups to purchase an annuity because their accumulated savings are likely to be very low and the terms currently offered by annuity providers are geared to the profile of wealthier retirees, who are likely to live longer on average (Stewart, 2007).

Unfunded individual accounts – otherwise known as notional defined contribution (NDC) arrangements[4] – provide a possible alternative to funded schemes. NDC plans resemble traditional defined contribution arrangements in the sense that contributors accumulate an entitlement but differ from a funded system in two important respects: 1) the interest rate is set by government rules (NDC plans are public programmes), not by market returns, and 2) the accumulation is only notional, in the sense that the system is not fully funded and may be entirely based on a pay-as-you-go (PAYG) system. At retirement, the value of the worker's notional accumulation is converted into an annuity in a way that mimics actuarial principles: benefits over the worker's expected remaining lifetime are set equal in present value to the worker's notional accumulation, using the notional interest rate as the discount rate.

NDC arrangements do not require a large pool of savings, which means that the transition costs of switching from a defined benefit scheme are very low (though unfunded pension schemes imply a debt which must be borne by future generations). They also operate without the need for an annuity market. An NDC scheme might therefore be appropriate for a newly established pension arrangement in contexts where capital markets are not sufficiently developed. The notional interest rate is governed by a set of economic and demographic factors and thus represents an automatic safeguard of sustainability. NDC schemes are a relatively new innovation; to date they have been implemented in four OECD countries (Italy, Latvia, Poland and Sweden),[5] as well as in Russia, Azerbaijan and Kyrgyzstan.

Figure 3.3. **Male and female labour force participation – proportion of population aged 15-64**

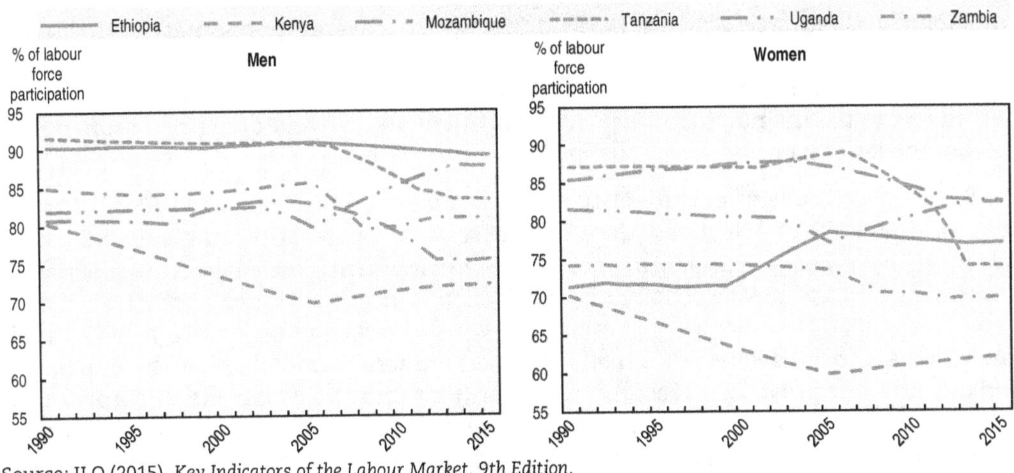

Source: ILO (2015), *Key Indicators of the Labour Market, 9th Edition.*

Future social insurance arrangements must promote gender equity. Traditional social insurance arrangements often place women at a disadvantage. The gender pay gap that prevails in most countries, the lower labour force participation among women (Figure 3.3) and the greater likelihood that women will be engaged in domestic work or unpaid care work are just a few of the reasons that limit the duration and value of their contributions to such schemes. Moreover, women are less likely to have access to assets and what wealth they do possess in retirement has to last longer than in the case of men due to women's relative longevity. Providing care credits for women whose pension contributions are interrupted as a result of childrearing has proven successful in improving pensions received by women in Chile. However, for women operating outside formal employment, non-contributory pensions are likely to remain an essential protection from poverty.

A final word of caution is required as countries across Africa look to scale up their social insurance schemes: the expansion of such arrangements in a context of high informality needs to be managed carefully to avoid generating a vicious circle whereby informality worsens and tax revenues decline. The experience of Latin America, where social security contributions account for almost the entire tax wedge between the cost of employment and a worker's take-home pay in many countries, shows how social security contributions create the same distortions as other labour taxes and thus have the same (potentially adverse) implications for employment and economic growth (OECD, CIAT and IDB, 2016). High contribution rates incentivise employers to hire informally, which not only leaves these workers reliant on state support in the event of loss of income but also reduces the resources available to the government to provide this support. In order to avoid such a situation, it is important to understand *ex ante* the behavioural responses of employers and employees to different contribution rates, as well as the capacity of workers at different income levels to contribute to social insurance arrangements.

Public works programmes can help to meet the employment challenge

Chapter 2 illustrated how difficult it will be for labour markets across the six countries to absorb new entrants over the next 50 years. Public works programmes (PWPs) will make a crucial contribution in meeting the employment challenge confronting East Africa. These arrangements, which use labour-intensive methods to provide public goods, are already being implemented in the region through Ethiopia's Productive Safety Net Programme (PSNP), the Tanzanian Social Action Fund (TASAF) and Rwanda's Vision 2020 Umurenge Programme. The experience of India's Mahatma Ghandi National Rural Employment Guarantee Scheme (MGNREGS), which covers approximately 50 million households and operates at a cost of just 0.5% of GDP (McCartney and Roy, 2016), shows that such programmes can operate at far larger scale than they are at present. However, PWPs need to meet a number of key criteria if they are to avoid doing more harm than good in the long term.

First, policy makers must identify and prioritise the objectives of PWPs. PWPs can achieve a number of objectives: they can serve as a source of income support (social safety net), as a means of promoting productive employment (active labour market policy) or as a cost-effective means of delivering public goods in a constrained fiscal environment (Devereux, 2002). However, they cannot achieve all three simultaneously. A PWP that is intended as a social safety net is likely to target vulnerable members of the population and prioritise the provision of income, while one that acts as a labour-market programme will target working-age individuals and place greater emphasis on the type of work that is performed and on the skills that participants acquire. Policy makers must recognise how these different objectives interact within a given programme, prioritise between them and reflect these choices in its design and financing arrangements.

PWPs need to be targeted, rationed and linked to complementary initiatives to maximise their impact. It is neither financially feasible for PWPs to act as a perpetual source of employment for the same individual nor is it desirable from a labour-market perspective. To prevent PWPs from representing only a temporary (McCord, 2012) response to the challenges of poverty and joblessness, mechanisms must be included in the design of a programme to limit the duration of participation and to connect participants to complementary programmes that offer a sustainable livelihood or source of income.

The evidence presented in this report indicates that PWPs should be targeted primarily at young people, should prioritise the provision of training that is aligned to the demands of the labour market, and should link participants to livelihood initiatives. PWPs whose principal objective is to provide income support to vulnerable groups should over time give way to cash transfer schemes, which are a more straightforward and cost-effective means of doing so. The Fourth round of the PSNP (to be implemented between 2016 and 2020) distinguishes between participants in public works and beneficiaries with no labour capacity. Public works participants and direct support recipients comprise 83% and 17% of PSNP beneficiaries respectively (Republic of Ethiopia, 2016).

There must be co-ordination and clear allocation of roles between central and local government. A common challenge to scaling up public works programmes is how to manage the balance between national and regional spheres of government. It is very challenging for a centralised programme to identify what would constitute useful work at the local level (Box 3.4). A centralised programme also faces a huge administrative burden that encompasses not only the registering and payment of participants but also ensuring the smooth running and effective outputs of individual projects. As a result, local governments need to play an active role in the implementation of PWPs and therefore require the resources and capacity to do so. However, national governments need to co-ordinate the programme as a whole, oversee monitoring and evaluation and ensure adequate financing.

Box 3.4. **Useful work – a core concept of the PSNP and TASAF**

Ethiopia and Tanzania are already incorporating large-scale public works programmes into their social protection systems. The Productive Safety Net Programme (PSNP) in Ethiopia and the Productive Social Safety Net component of TASAF combine targeted cash transfers with public works programmes that employ poor participants to provide assets to their broader community during the agricultural lean season. Both programmes are in the process of expanding and evolving: the PSNP now benefits close to 8 million individuals (or close to 8% of the population) and the Ethiopian government is in the process of designing an urban variant, while TASAF is significantly expanding into a greater number of districts after a successful pilot.

The rapid expansion of the PSNP and TASAF are testament to the strength and scalability of the model; it is very likely that other countries in Africa and elsewhere will follow the model in response to their own employment challenges. While adaptation to local contexts is necessary, a key aspect of the public works components of the PSNP and TASAF that must be retained is their emphasis on generating assets that enhance communities' economic potential or boost their resilience to climate-related and other shocks that might threaten their livelihoods.

> **Box 3.4. Useful work – a core concept of the PSNP and TASAF** (cont.)
>
> This focus on "useful work" is important for countering a typical criticism of PWPs, namely that the work they perform does not have any real value and the costs associated with any such work are therefore a waste of money. The principal criticism levelled at the MGNREGS is that the assets generated through the scheme are of very low quality. Ensuring that the work performed by such programmes will be of value to the community and will not fall into disrepair once a project is completed requires that the community is involved with the process to select the project, that the type of project aligns not only to the skill level of participants but also to the type of tools and equipment at their disposal, and that a maintenance plan is established before the project ends.

If PWPs can create assets of sufficient quality, they should be linked to broader development strategies such as public infrastructure plans, agriculture policies, urban development or industrial policy. There is clear scope for mutually beneficial outcomes: PWPs support these plans through the provision of relatively low-cost labour while the ministries responsible for implementing these plans support the success of the PWPs by providing relevant technical expertise. This model allows for considerable diversification in the types of projects performed by public works programmes, as South Africa's Expanded Public Works Programme (EPWP) is already showing (Box 3.5).

> **Box 3.5. The value of diversification in South Africa's Expanded Public Works Programme**
>
> Since its establishment in 2004, the EPWP has broadened its scope from focusing predominantly on infrastructure to environmental projects (such as safeguarding water supplies and waste management) and social services, including home and community-based care, school-feeding and early childhood development. The EPWP also supports the work of non-government organisations (often working in the social sector) by subsidising their employment costs.
>
> The provision of social services has clear multiplier effects for poor communities: they not only provide work to unemployed people (typically women), but this work also provides services that might otherwise be unavailable to the communities. Moreover, moving the burden of care from the household to the community level is an important means of empowering women who currently devote the majority of their time to caring for household members to pursue economic activities.
>
> This diversification of activities means that unlike other large-scale public works programmes the EPWP has a strong urban footprint and can provide work all year round. They can also be an answer to infrastructure issues and service delivery challenges in rapidly growing urban centres.

The design of large-scale PWPs should minimise distortions of the labour market. Analysis of MGNREGS has demonstrated how large-scale public employment programmes affect wages and labour supply in the "formal" economy in areas where they are implemented, though this effect is partly mitigated by the fact the scheme is only implemented during the agricultural lean season (Varshney, Goel and Meenakshi, 2014). If rolled out at a sufficiently large scale, PWPs might distort the overall productivity of a country's economy by employing a significant proportion of the labour force in work that is chosen by government and is not necessarily optimal for the development of the economy or for the individuals themselves in terms of their acquisition of skills. The Community Work Programme in South Africa, a public employment programme that provides work to participants all year round, seeks to limit this impact by rationing employment to two days a week, freeing up time for participants to seek employment in the formal labour market.

Large-scale PWPs risk undermining the rights and conditions of workers in the "formal" economy if public agencies use these schemes as a low-cost substitute to the private-sector contractors they would ordinarily use. Close co-operation between government and labour organisations is important to avoid such a situation. PWPs must be made equally accessible to women as to men, for example by designating tasks that women can be reasonably expected to perform and through the provision of childcare facilities at worksites. It is also important to provide participants with access to social insurance arrangements, as is done in by South Africa's EPWP, whose participants contribute to the unemployment insurance fund and are enrolled in a workers compensation scheme.

Rapid urbanisation calls for innovation in social protection delivery

Urban social protection programmes are poorly developed but demand for such programmes will grow across the sample countries. World Bank data show that social assistance programmes globally cover 15.4% of poor households,[6] versus 25.1% in rural areas. While the rate of monetary poverty might be lower in cities than in rural areas, general levels of deprivation between the two areas can be similar in magnitude, as discussed in Chapter 1. A recent study by the OECD shows that inequality of income and other wellbeing indicators is a particular problem in urban areas (OECD, 2016b). East Africa's rapid urbanisation – its urban population will increase by a multiple of four by 2050 – will require social protection planners to rethink their strategies and redesign their programmes. Ethiopia is leading the way in terms of adapting social protection to urban areas with the expected launch of the Urban Productive Safety Net Programme in 2017 (Box 3.6).

As Chapter 1 notes, there is a major information deficit concerning the nature, extent and dynamics of urban poverty, especially in slums. Designing and implementing an appropriate social protection arrangement in these circumstances is extremely challenging. In general terms, urban areas are associated with higher individual mobility than rural areas, as well as greater fluctuations in income, both of which make it harder to target or even reach beneficiaries; promoting equitable access under such conditions is likely to push up administrative costs. The cost of living in urban areas also tends to be higher, particularly in terms of food, housing and transport. This requires adjustments to benefit levels relative to schemes in rural areas, placing further upwards pressure on the cost of urban programmes.

The high levels of multi-dimensional poverty in urban areas relative to monetary poverty indicates that social protection programmes might need to prioritise access to basic and social services over income support. However, such services need to exist and be accessible in the first place. Chapter 1 notes that most of the growth in urban areas will take place in towns and cities that are presently no more than villages or small towns, meaning they lack infrastructure, administrative capacity and adequate financial resources to provide public services.

The use of PWPs to support provision of infrastructure and services can be an important means of reconciling the imperatives of poverty alleviation and the provision of services. Enlisting local communities to provide care for children and other vulnerable household members has great potential as a means of overcoming the information and resource constraints faced by local administrations.

> **Box 3.6. Extending social protection to urban areas: Ethiopia's forthcoming Urban PSNP**
>
> In 2017, Ethiopia is expected to launch the Urban PSNP in a number of cities across the country. Although details of the programme have not yet been finalised, its design is likely to differ in a number of important ways from the existing PSNP. The Urban PSNP will be part of what the World Bank refers to as a "first generation" of urban social protection programmes around the world (Gentilini, 2015). There is considerable variation between these, but their common objective is to alleviate poverty and mitigate inequality, while at the same time connecting individuals to services, enhancing human capital and promoting economic activity. As their cities continue to grow, the other countries in this sample will need to follow the lessons learned from this first generation and adapt them to their own contexts.
>
> *Source:* Gentilini (2015), "Entering the City: Emerging Evidence and Practices with Safety Nets in Urban Areas".

Placing social protection at the fore of climate-change adaptation strategies

Social protection is emerging as a key instrument in adapting to the unpredictable and varied threat to livelihoods posed by climate change. As discussed in Chapter 1, climate change will have a significant impact on the East African region. However, the precise nature of this impact will not be predictable in terms of its timing, location or severity. Where rising temperatures and higher sea levels will lead to gradual changes in rural productivity and therefore require a longer-term adaptation strategy, droughts and cyclones take a rapid toll and require a quicker response. Social protection interventions have long been an important part of the policy response to disasters, but they need to be part of a mitigation strategy through instruments that are as broad and diverse as the nature of the threat itself.

Social protection can support climate change adaptation, helping individuals to diversify their livelihoods and communities to "climate-proof" their land and infrastructure in response to climate-related threats. The PSNP and TASAF have both integrated climate change mitigation into their design: both programmes prioritise public works projects that enhance communities' resilience to climate change as part of a long-term strategy to increase agricultural productivity. Enhancing resilience *ex ante* reduces the need for reactive measures. Emergency aid can be expensive, slow to arrive and unable to reach the places most in need. Evacuation is also expensive, not only for public authorities but also for the households forced to abandon their land and possessions.

An important part of the *ex ante* response is to link social protection programmes to early warning systems for food security (del Ninno, Coll-Black and Fallavier, 2016; Devereux, 2003). Kenya's Hunger Safety Net Programme (HSNP), which operates in food-insecure arid and semi-arid regions in the north of the country, has demonstrated the potential for linking social protection programmes not only to respond to a climate shock but also to anticipate one. Confronted by drought conditions in 2015, the programme was able to scale up rapidly by an additional 100 000 households because it has already registered and provided bank accounts to people who lived in areas covered by the scheme but were not yet eligible for benefits. Moreover, the HSNP was able to make a special transfer to 200 000 households in anticipation of a drought occurring later in the same year (Hallegatte et al., 2017).

In its 2016 report on the impact of climate change on poverty, the World Bank echoes Agenda 2063 in recognising the central role that microinsurance can play in allowing low-income individuals to protect themselves against the impact of climate change (World Bank, 2015a). East Africa is making important progress in this regard: in 2016, the governments of both Kenya and Ethiopia launched national programmes enabling small-scale farmers to insure themselves against weather-related shocks (World Bank, 2016b; Ethiopian News Agency, 2016). In the same year, the Ugandan government also launched a programme to subsidise farmers' insurance premiums (Batte, 2016).

Although rural households are likely to bear the brunt of climate change in East Africa, the phenomenon will have direct consequences for urban populations as well. With rural-to-urban migration likely to intensify in response to acute climate shocks, pressure on urban labour markets and demand for urban social protection programmes will also rise. At the same time, weather-related shocks can have a major adverse impact on food security, pushing up prices and reducing its availability. Urban social protection programmes will need to incorporate scalability and responsiveness to such challenges into their design.

Securing a demographic dividend by empowering women and providing for children and the elderly

The fertility decline has stalled across the six countries, implying that population growth will continue at its present level. This would be disastrous for the countries' attempts to reduce poverty and promote development. The potential for a demographic dividend would disappear, especially in a context where a large proportion of the workforce is likely to be engaged in low-productivity work.

Social protection has a key role to play in empowering women and there exists overwhelming evidence that women's empowerment – both in terms of resources and agency – is associated with lower levels of fertility. Empowerment not only means women staying longer in school and increasing their labour force participation, but it also means women being more involved in household decision-making. The impact of policies to empower women can be rapid and significant: Ferré (2009) shows that an additional year of female schooling in Kenya is associated with a 10% reduction in the fertility rate.

A perception exists that targeting cash transfers at the mothers of young children incentivises them to have more children. Recent evidence from Kenya and Zambia shows the contrary to be true. An evaluation of Kenya's Cash Transfer for Orphans and Vulnerable Children by Handa et al. (2015) shows that receipt of the transfer reduced the likelihood of pregnancy among 12-24 year olds by five percentage points (or 34%). Meanwhile, Palermo et al. (2016) demonstrate that the Zambian Child Grant was associated with a lower likelihood of pregnancy among young women. Both transfers were unconditional.

There are various channels through which receipt of the grants in Kenya and Zambia might have affected fertility decisions among young women. A global survey of cash transfer programmes by the Overseas Development Institute shows how such interventions have been associated with higher school attendance and improved learning outcomes among girls, lower rates of female child employment, higher labour force participation among adult women, and an increase in asset ownership, savings and investment (Bastagli et al., 2016). Receipt of a cash transfer is also associated with lower levels of female abuse and a positive impact on women's choices regarding fertility, marriage and engagement in sexual activity. FAO (2015) highlights how social protection can empower women in rural areas but emphasises the importance of linking beneficiaries to complementary livelihoods initiatives and services to maximise the potential impact.

Improving women's access to health services, and to family planning clinics in particular, is perhaps the most direct mechanism for reducing fertility. As a result, family planning services should be included in basic health packages available at no cost to all citizens, as happens through Ethiopia's Health Extension Programme, which has significantly increased access to health services among low-income households (UNICEF, 2016). The design of these facilities matters: if a clinic distinguishes between family planning services and maternal and child health services, for example, the stigma attached to contraception in a given society might deter women from using the former.

Social protection interventions that are not aimed at women can also cause significant reductions in fertility. It has been found in a wide variety of contexts that the provision of pensions has contributed to declines in fertility because these instruments weaken the motivation for parents to have children to provide a means of support when they get old. Holmqvist (2010) found that the effect holds in South Africa, Mauritius, Seychelles, Namibia, Botswana, Lesotho and Swaziland, all of which have implemented non-contributory social pension schemes with coverage in excess of 80% of the eligible population. The provision of old age pensions in South Africa has been found to promote school attendance among children in the same household as the pension recipient, meaning this grant has an impact similar to the country's Child Support Grant (Budlender and Woolard, 2006). This underlines the importance of adopting a lifecycle approach to the provision of social protection, whereby an intervention principally designed for one point in the life cycle can also address risks identified at another.

An individual's productivity is (to a great extent) determined long before they start work. Social protection has been shown to promote human capital development by enhancing enrolment in school but there is scope for productive investment even before children reach that age. Cognitive development during the pre-school years has been shown to have a greater impact than education and training at a later age (Carneiro and Heckman, 2003). Investment in early childhood development (ECD) can promote cognitive development among the youngest age cohorts and thus promote productivity in later life. At the individual level, such schemes are a means of breaking the inter-generational transmission of poverty and promoting social mobility; at the aggregate level, these gains will enhance productivity across the economy. Although evidence on the impact of ECD interventions in developing countries is scarce, Gertler et al. (2014) demonstrated that the average incomes of individuals who benefited from an ECD scheme in Jamaica during the 1980s were 25% higher than those of a control group 20 years later.

There are many dimensions to ECD, which encompass health, nutrition, education and access to basic services and which involve both formal and informal facilities as well as the home (Britto et al., 2017). These different interventions need to be integrated within a coherent policy framework under the purview of social protection. Looking specifically at one component of ECD – pre-primary enrolment – we see this is significantly lower than gross primary enrolment for the four countries for which data is available (Figure 3.4). In Kenya, enrolment grew strongly between 2005 and 2014 from a base that was already significantly higher than in the other countries. Enrolment is also rising in Ethiopia, while a flatter trend is identified in Tanzania and Uganda, the other two countries for which data is available. Kenya has enjoyed great success in promoting pre-school services since independence in 1963 through the Harambee initiative, a partnership between the government, families and communities (World Bank, 2008).

Figure 3.4. Pre-primary school gross enrolment ratio, 2005-14

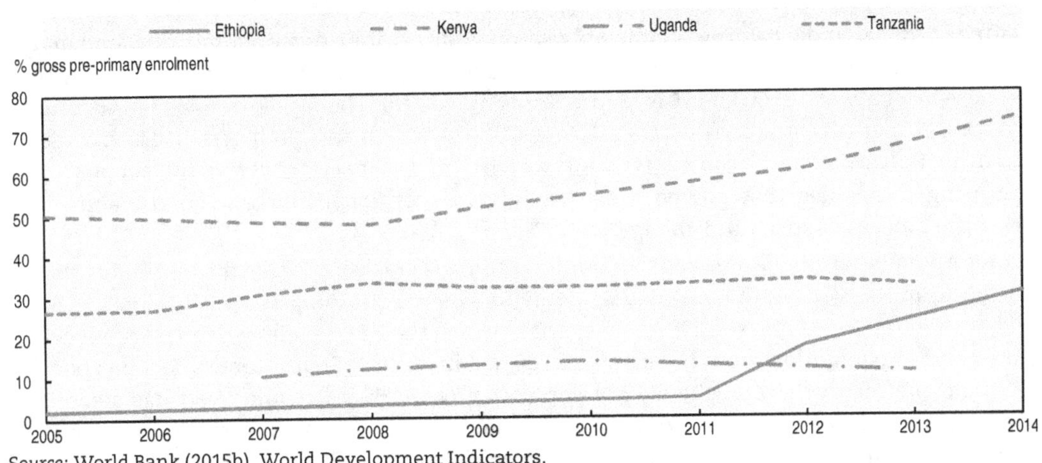

Source: World Bank (2015b), World Development Indicators.

As noted in Chapter 2, domestic savings across the six countries do not match the amount needed for investment, forcing them to rely on external capital flows. This situation might change as the dependency ratio falls: a higher proportion of producers relative to consumers is likely to increase the level of savings at an economy-wide level, an effect reinforced by the impact of rising life expectancies on income-smoothing behaviour. This increase in savings can promote investment in physical capital and thus facilitate capital widening and deepening. This is not only an important means of harnessing the potential of large working-age population but also acts as a pre-emptive mechanism for mitigating less favourable demographic conditions associated with population ageing: when the labour force shrinks relative to the number of old-age dependants, productivity per worker must increase to maintain the same level of output. These two effects are sometimes referred to as the first and second demographic dividend.

Poverty acts as a major brake on savings, resulting in a strong correlation at a national level between income per capita and the savings rate. So too does a lack of financial inclusion. Social protection can play a dual role in promoting savings. First, it can reduce poverty. Secondly, it can incentivise saving by providing a publicly administered savings vehicle (typically, a pension fund) which compels people to save and which overcomes challenges related to financial inclusion. Domestic investment might increase as a result, though a positive relationship between pensions, savings and investment is not guaranteed: many countries in Latin America have established funded individual account arrangements but only in Chile and Peru have there been clear benefits in terms of increased national savings or capital market development.

Box 3.7. How South Korea crafted and captured a demographic dividend

In East Asia, the fertility decline was accompanied by rapid economic growth and strong advances in human development indicators between 1960 and 1990. However, it was not until 1997 that the possibility of an explicit link between the region's economic performance and the changes to the countries' age structure was explored. Bloom and Williamson's paper Demographic Transitions and Economic Miracles in Emerging Asia (1997) calculated that between a third and a half of overall growth in the region's GDP per capita between 1965 and 1990 could be attributed to population dynamics.

Box 3.7. **How South Korea crafted and captured a demographic dividend** (cont.)

South Korea is considered a prime example of how to manufacture a demographic dividend and exploit its potential through interventions in family planning, public health and education. In just over 50 years, between 1960 and 2014, South Korea moved from being a low- to a high-income country: its GDP per capita rose from USD 156 to USD 27 221 in real 2014 terms. Meanwhile, it adopted an industrial development strategy which lent extensive government support to manufacturing companies that proved their viability in the global market, thereby actively promoting the process of structural change.

South Korea's population policies helped the country attain a rapid decline in fertility and mortality rates shortly after the war. South Korea had implemented family planning as a population control method between the 1960s and the 1990s, which has caused the TFR to fall by five and produced a large reversal in population growth during the 2000s. Since 1984, South Korea's TFR has been under 2.0 and the relative size of the elderly population (aged 65 years and over) has steadily increased since the 1970s (UN DESA, 2015). By 1983, the country had attained a replacement level fertility rate; as of 2012, it was 1.21, the lowest in the world.

South Korea achieved universal health insurance in 12 years. Starting in 1963, legislation helped open health-insurance access to the populace. At first, health insurance was administered on a voluntary basis. The first mandate for health insurance came in 1977 but only for the employees of large companies and their dependents. Subsequently, the government mandated health insurance access for government employees and private school teachers, and by 1989, health insurance had been extended to the entire population, with co-payment. Universal coverage was rapidly achieved by limiting the range of benefits covered by the National Health Insurance (NHI), although coverage has broadened over time, and by fixing medical prices at low levels (Jones, 2010).

What is today one of the best systems of education in the world developed rapidly. Following the war, the government centralised control of education and passed a number of reforms that aimed to develop a literate and skilled electorate. Widespread illiteracy was eliminated by the mid-60s and as of 2013, 92.4% of the cohort completes upper secondary education – among the highest in the OECD. South Korea's education policy is aligned to its broader innovation policy, which has been a key growth driver over the last 30 years. The country's strategic approach to science, technology, and innovation has required and, through tailored education policies, created a highly-skilled workforce. Korea's vision for a knowledge-based economy is highly dependent on its education policies and technology investments in basic science R&D.

Bloom and Williamson's identification of a "demographic gift" in East Asia has created an expectation that countries that are lagging the region in terms of the fertility transition can achieve comparable success through policies similar to those adopted in East Asia. While there are important lessons to derive from the East Asian example, it is unrealistic to assume that the experience can be automatically replicated in a different place and time.

Note: Definitions of East Africa for the purposes of discussing the region's economic transformation are often guided by the World Bank's report "The East Asian Miracle: Economic Growth and Public Policy" (1993). The included countries are typically classified as South-East Asian within East Asia and created a separate sub-group comprising eight "High-Performing Asian Economies" (HPAEs): Hong Kong, Singapore, South Korea and Taiwan (the four "Tigers"), Japan, Indonesia, Malaysia and Thailand.

Sources: Bloom and Williamson (1997), "Demographic Transitions and Economic Miracles in Emerging Asia"; Jones (2010), "Health-care Reform in Korea"; UN DESA (2015), *World Population Prospects: The 2015 Revision*; World Bank (2015c), *Ethiopia Poverty Assessment 2014*, Report No. AUS6744.

Expanding the social protection budget without hurting the poor

The economies of the six countries studied here have performed strongly in the recent past, increasing the resources available for social protection. Nonetheless, governments across the six sample countries need to raise a much higher level of taxes as a proportion of GDP to address the multiple challenges they face.

Agenda 2063 states that spending on social protection across Africa needs to rise from its present average of 2% of GDP to 5% of GDP. IMF data (Figure 3.5) illustrates the implications of such an increase. With the exception of Mozambique, the sample countries generate tax revenues within a range of 10% of GDP (Uganda) to 16% of GDP (Kenya): an increase in spending on social protection that was financed by taxation alone would require revenues to increase as a percentage of GDP by between 19% and 33%.

Such a step change in revenue generation will take time and huge political will to achieve. In the short- to medium-term, financing strategies for social protection need to combine improvements to the tax system with reforms on the expenditure side that maximise the impact of existing social protection or pro-poor spending. This section identifies possible reforms to the tax system and expenditure in turn.

Figure 3.5. **Tax revenue as a percentage of GDP, 2000-13**

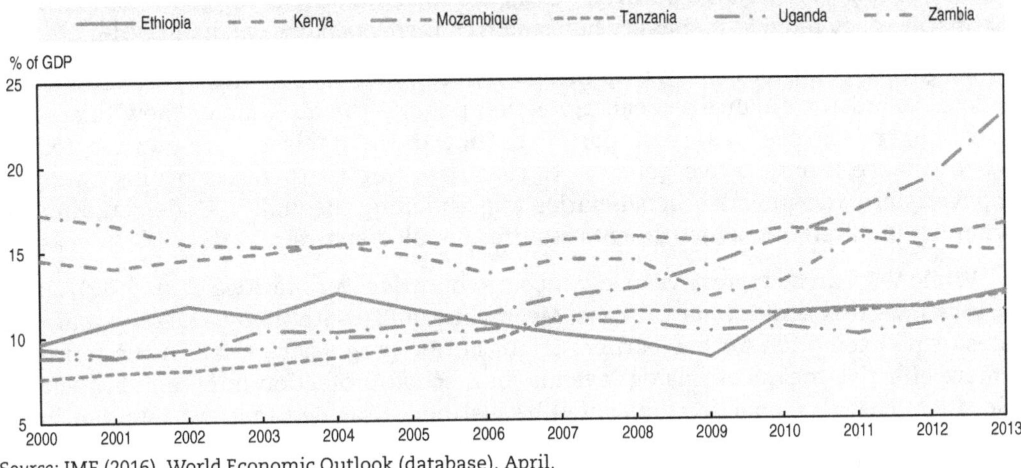

Source: IMF (2016), World Economic Outlook (database), April.

Improving the tax system

Developing a social protection system requires sources of financing that are sustainable over a long time horizon. This requirement limits the extent to which two important sources of income for many African countries – Official Development Assistance (ODA) and natural resource revenues – can provide a significant portion of the revenue mix over the long term. Flagship social protection schemes across the six countries (including PSNP, TASAF and the Social Cash Transfer in Zambia) rely on ODA (in the form of grants and concessional lending) for a considerable proportion of their financing. However, donor support is volatile and can be expected to decline as per capita incomes increase in the six countries. The governments of Ethiopia and Tanzania are already promoting increased domestic financing for PSNP and TASAF respectively. It is in the interests of donors and recipients alike to manage the tapering of external assistance through a clear long-term strategy.

Natural resources across East Africa are thought to be abundant, though exploration has so far been limited. Tax revenues in developing countries with substantial natural resources tend to be higher than for countries at the same income level that lack such resources. However, this does not necessarily place them at an advantage in terms of financing social protection programmes: fluctuations in commodity prices and the finite nature of such resources limits their capacity to provide the reliable and sustainable revenue flows on which social programmes depend.

Governments' ability to raise taxes on companies and individuals will be essential to reaching the 5% target. However, the projections in Chapter 2 underscore the challenge that lies ahead in this regard. The persistence of agricultural and informal employment as the mainstays of the labour market even 50 years from now will make it harder to generate revenues through direct taxation in the form of personal income tax (PIT) or corporate income tax (CIT) – instruments that can be aimed at those who can most easily bear the burden of taxation.

As a result, governments continue to rely on indirect taxes, such as value added tax on consumption (which accounts for about 25% of tax revenues in developing countries) and excise duties, the burden of which falls on all consumers (IMF, 2011). With Chapter 2 also demonstrating that a significant proportion of the individuals and households will remain poor and vulnerable for some time to come, increasing taxes on consumption risks pushing people (further) into poverty. Recent evidence for developing countries confirms that fiscal policy reduces inequality but can often increase poverty (Lustig, 2016).

As governments look to scale up their revenues – and particularly if they are looking to do so in order to finance a social protection policy – the question of "how" a specific instrument raises revenues is as important as "how much" it raises. To rely on a regressive tax to finance a progressive policy is to risk offsetting the benefits of this policy by impoverishing the intended beneficiaries and widening inequality. Understanding the dynamics of different tax instruments requires detailed analysis.

While VAT can be regressive in low-income countries (Peralta-Alva et al., 2017), Lustig (2016) shows this is often not the case. Meanwhile, a PIT with non-graduating marginal rates or no exemption for low earners might not be progressive at all. If the former is a more effective means of raising revenue for a social protection intervention then the additional cost to a poor consumer will be justified, provided that the intervention is sufficiently generous and well targeted to offset this cost.

Fiscal incidence analysis (Box 3.8) is an essential means of understanding who bears the burden from the different instruments upon which domestic resource mobilisation depends. It also shows the overall impact on poverty and demonstrates the extent to which individuals along the income distribution are either net payers or net beneficiaries from a system of taxes and transfers. The importance of simultaneously examining both the spending and the revenue side of the fiscal framework requires social policy makers to be more involved in discussions around tax – traditionally the sole purview of Finance Ministries – than they typically are today.

Across the six countries, indirect taxes contribute a much larger proportion of total tax revenues than direct taxes on income and profits (PIT or CIT). Increasing revenues from PIT and CIT holds the key to domestic resource mobilisation but there are major challenges to doing so. In the case of PIT, high levels of informality and self-employment in developing countries impose significant constraints on enforcement.

Attempts to increase CIT not only encounter problems with enforcement among domestic enterprises operating in the informal sector but also confront sophisticated tax avoidance strategies adopted by multinational corporations, which exploit loopholes in the international tax system to significantly reduce their obligations in countries where they are active. Crivelli, Mooij and Keen (2015) calculate that these practices cost developing countries 1.3% of GDP, which is higher than the losses incurred by OECD countries (1.0% of GDP), represents a greater proportion of total tax revenues raised and exceeds the average expenditure on social assistance across the six countries. An objective of the Base Erosion and Profit Shifting (BEPS) initiative, an international effort led by the OECD and G20, is to enhance developing countries' ability to levy CIT from multinational companies (OECD, 2015).

Box 3.8. Fiscal incidence analysis in Ethiopia, Tanzania and Uganda

The Commitment to Equity Institute (CEQI) has developed a methodology for analysing the combined impact of taxes and social spending on a country's income distribution and poverty level in an internationally comparable manner. The methodology reconciles survey data with administrative and national accounts data for a given year. It includes social protection schemes and monetises in-kind benefits from public health and education services. Among the 23 counties where CEQI has applied this methodology, three are in this sample: Ethiopia, Tanzania and Uganda (World Bank, 2015c; Younger et al., 2016; Jellema et al., 2016).

For Ethiopia (based on data from 2011), this analysis showed that the PSNP reduced poverty by 2% but that the design of the tax system (in particular the PIT for low-income earners and agricultural taxes) partly offset these gains. In 2016, the Ethiopian government raised the minimum monthly earnings threshold for PIT from 150 Birr (USD 6.63) to 585 Birr and adjusted the tax schedule at other income levels in order to reduce the tax burden on the poor and make the tax more progressive.

For Tanzania (using 2011/12 data), taxes (both direct and indirect) are shown to be progressive but the low coverage of cash transfers meant that even the extreme poor were "net payers" to the fiscus and the overall effect of taxes and transfers was to increase poverty. In-kind health and education benefits more than offset this effect, such that the overall fiscal impact was to reduce poverty by 3.3 percentage points.

In Uganda (using 2012/13 data), social spending (and the fiscal system as a whole) is shown to be too small to make a significant impact on either poverty or inequality. The absence of a large cash transfer scheme and high coverage of indirect taxes result in poor households being net payers to the fiscal system.

As countries look to scale up their social protection systems, this kind of analysis provides valuable evidence as to which programmes are most effective in reducing poverty and inequality and which taxes (including social insurance arrangements) impose the least burden on the poor. However, the methodology cannot be used to model the impact of a specific tax or spending reform because it does not capture the general equilibrium effects of such a measure.

Sources: World Bank (2015c), *Ethiopia Poverty Assessment 2014*, Report No. AUS6744; Jellema et al. (2016) "The Impact of Taxes, Transfers, and Subsidies on Inequality and Poverty in Uganda"; Younger et al. (2016), "Fiscal incidence in Tanzania," African Development Review 28(3), pp. 264–276.

Developing countries globally are failing to maximise the potential of taxes from immovable property as a means of financing urban services. Bahl, Martinez-Vazquez and Youngman (2010) calculate that revenues from immovable property taxes in developing countries equated to 0.6% of GDP in the 2000s versus 2.1% of GDP in OECD countries over the same period. In East Africa, immovable property taxes are especially underdeveloped and have been very unpopular historically (Fjeldstad, Chambas and Brun, 2014), though Mozambique and Rwanda are currently undertaking reforms to improve their impact (Kopanyi, 2015).

The benefits of increasing these taxes in a context of rapid urbanisation would be considerable, especially in terms of financing social and basic services. Moreover, these taxes are equitable and promote accountability at the local government sphere, since the link between tax payments and benefits received is much more visible than at the national sphere. However, important constraints exist to levying these taxes in developing countries, including the maturity of property markets, a lack of information regarding property prices and weak administrative capacity within local government. Moreover, without a significant degree of fiscal decentralisation, the incentive for local governments to implement property taxes is significantly diminished (Bahl, Martinez-Vazquez and Youngman, 2010).

Enhancing the tax system by improving revenue generation and increasing administrative capacity is vital for financing social protection. However, the benefits are not solely financial. For example, contributory social insurance arrangements can achieve efficiency gains by piggy-backing on the tax system in order to collect pension and unemployment insurance contributions. Indeed, it is difficult to establish social insurance arrangements without a certain level of tax administration capacity and without a significant degree of compliance.

However, the benefits are not just one-way: a tax increase to a specific social intervention – as when Ghana linked a VAT increase to an expansion of health insurance and the Philippines raised sin taxes for the same purpose – has been an important means of securing popular support for tax increases. Tax morale and compliance will typically improve if populations believe their taxes are being spent in a responsible and fair manner.

There is a strong case for international development partners to substantially increase support for countries to develop their tax administration capacity. Expenditure on such projects accounted for just over 0.1% of total ODA in 2010 but the associated returns can exceed those generated by many other, better-resourced interventions (IMF, OECD, UN and WBG, 2016).

Maximising the impact of existing social protection or pro-poor spending

The six countries studied in this report subsidise food, fuel and electricity through a variety of mechanisms. The rationale for these subsidies is often that they safeguard the ability of poor households to access essential goods. However, these subsidies are widely found to be regressive: according to the IMF, 45% of the value of fuel subsidies in sub-Saharan Africa accrues to the wealthiest consumption quintile, while only 10% of households in the lowest two quintiles in the region even have access to electricity and thus benefit from the subsidised prices (Alleyne and Hussain, 2013). The World Bank (2008) found there to be substantial leakage of food subsidies to higher-income groups, since these households also consume the subsidised staples, and in larger absolute quantities.

Replacing or eliminating these subsidies would free up significant resources for governments to spend on social protection programmes aimed directly at supporting the consumption of poor households. Table 3.2 shows the scale of the potential savings generated by eliminating energy subsidies across the six countries, which range from 1.5% of GDP in Uganda to 8.3% of GDP in Zambia. Increasing expenditure on social protection by equivalent amounts in the respective countries would not only achieve major gains in terms of reducing poverty and inequality[7] but would also lead to broader efficiency gains, in particular in terms of incentivising electricity producers to enhance their distribution networks (Alleyne and Hussain, 2013). Eliminating fuel subsidies might also yield environmental benefits by reducing emissions.

Removing subsidies is often very challenging in political terms. Examining the removal of fuel subsidies in Ghana, Indonesia and Iran, Lindebjerg, Peng and Yeboah (2015) find that such reforms can generate a "triple win" (improved social distribution, fiscal savings and reduced emissions) but this is not guaranteed: subsidy reductions need to be carried out through a gradual and clearly-communicated process that emphasises the social benefits of the reform.

Table 3.2. **Fiscal savings after energy subsidy elimination**

	Post-tax subsidies as a percentage of GDP					Estimated total fiscal savings (USD billion)	Savings per capita (USD)
	Petroleum	Coal	Natural gas	Electricity	Total		
Ethiopia	2.0	0.1	0.0	1.1	3.2	1.63	18.38
Kenya	1.3	0.1	0.0	0.3	1.7	0.95	22.78
Mozambique	0.6	0.0	0.5	5.9	7.0	1.10	42.63
Tanzania	1.2	0.0	0.3	2.1	3.7	1.37	29.60
Uganda		0.0	0.0	1.5	1.5	0.38	10.52
Zambia	0.4	0.2	0.0	7.7	8.3	2.19	150.35

Source: IMF (2015), How large are global energy subsidies? (database), imf.org/external/pubs/ft/survey/so/2015/NEW070215A.htm

Humanitarian assistance and social protection are still widely viewed as discrete instruments. However, in regions that are vulnerable to extreme climatic conditions, there is a strong argument for bridging the gap between the two. As del Ninno et al. (2016) note, "Humanitarian assistance will remain an appropriate short-term response to emergencies, but in many countries it is provided year after year in the same areas and to the same recipients, suggesting it is being used as a long-term instrument to address chronic poverty". Social protection programmes represent a far more effective response in this regard, not only in terms of improving the outcomes for people living in those areas on a sustainable basis but also making more efficient use of funds.

Cabot Venton et al. (2012) demonstrate how the implementation of different mechanisms to enhance resilience to climate-related shocks in Kenya and Ethiopia would have proven more cost-effective than relying on humanitarian assistance, while del Ninno et al. (2016) demonstrate the affordability of scalable social protection programmes relative to humanitarian assistance across a number of countries. It is important to note, however, that budgeting for a scalable programme poses a challenge for public finance management, since it is not possible to predict *ex ante* when additional funds will be required or in what quantity (World Bank, 2015c; OECD, 2016c).

A third area where there is significant scope for reprioritisation of funds within the social protection spending envelope is pension arrangements for civil servants. As the World Bank notes, "Civil service pension spending in Africa may not appear high relative to other countries but it is extraordinarily high when we consider the number of people receiving pensions" (Schwarz and Abels, 2016). Expenditure per capita on such schemes is also notably high relative to other national social protection programmes: Tanzania, for example, spends 1.6% of GDP on its civil service pension scheme. About three quarters of civil service schemes across Africa are defined benefit arrangements run on a pay-as-you-go basis; in most cases, expenditures are financed by current employees and the government (the former through salary contributions, the latter through general tax revenues).

Civil service pension arrangements in the region typically offer higher accrual rates and earlier retirement ages than national schemes in their respective countries, and they are also more generous than equivalent schemes in OECD countries. Compounding this generosity is the fact that the age profile of civil service schemes is typically older than that of the country as a whole, meaning that population ageing is affecting these arrangements before it affects the wider population. This combination of generous benefits and rising dependency ratios is driving up expenditure at a rapid rate; with the government funding these benefits from general revenue, the cost of these entitlements is borne by the population as a whole and will absorb an ever-higher proportion of public spending.

The design of civil service schemes differs between the six sample countries. Mozambique, Tanzania and Uganda operate unfunded stand-alone schemes, while Ethiopia and Zambia have integrated civil servants into the public pension arrangements for the private sector and Kenya recently established a fully funded defined contribution arrangement for civil servants. Even if a reform process is under way, the legacy costs of old arrangements are extensive: entitlements for civil servants under the previous dispensation need to be honoured and the transition from an unfunded to a funded scheme imposes a significant debt on the government's balance sheet related to these entitlements.[8]

These legacy costs can be a convenient excuse not to enact policies that are likely to be unpopular with the constituency responsible for enacting them. However, with every year that passes, the long-term burden that civil service schemes represent magnifies; an urgent first step in the reform process is to quantify this liability through regular actuarial studies.

A final word on the need for better data

Social protection systems cannot function effectively without accurate and up-to-date information or systems that use this information. In sub-Saharan Africa, low statistics capacity has been a major challenge to understanding the dynamics of poverty and the impact of public policy in reducing poverty. As Beegle at al. (2016) note: "Problems with the availability, comparability, and quality of data, combined with different approaches and methods to correct for these shortcomings, are at the centre of the divergent views regarding the direction and magnitude of poverty reduction in Africa over the past two decades". Sub-Saharan Africa scored 60% in the World Bank's Bulletin Board on Statistical Capacity indicator in 2016, which is below the average of low-income countries (World Bank, 2015d). Of the six sample countries, Kenya and Zambia were below the regional average in 2016 while the other four countries were above this benchmark.

The first step in designing a social protection system is to understand the population it is intended to serve. Civil registration agencies are responsible for collecting a population's vital statistics - including births, deaths, marriages and adoptions – which can have immediate implications for the social protection system. This information is also important for keeping track of broader demographic trends such as population growth and life expectancy. At the same time, civil registration is necessary to ensure recognition of individuals' legal identity and a formal record of events such as births and deaths which might entitle them to essential services or social protection programmes. A study by the UN Statistics Division (UN DESA, 2016) showed civil-registration capacity to be generally weak across the six countries, with Kenya and Mozambique the better performers and Ethiopia and Zambia the weakest. In practical terms, this means that Ethiopia and Zambia rely on population censuses and sample data to generate basic vital statistics.

As Beegle et al. (2016) note, there has been a rapid increase in the number of household surveys conducted across Africa since the 1980s, which has generated data on a large number of indicators, including health, human development and subjective wellbeing. However, consumption surveys – which are essential for measuring monetary poverty – have not kept pace. This imposes a significant constraint on efforts to improve the effectiveness of social protection policies: consumption information is needed to assist with targeting interventions and to gauge their effectiveness. Household surveys which include specific social protection modules are obviously invaluable in this regard.

In order to establish a coherent social protection system, administrative data on individual social protection programmes needs to be combined within a single registry.[9] This information should cover the identity and quantity of beneficiaries in different schemes, disaggregated to the greatest extent possible by age, gender, region and other relevant information. It should also include the value of benefits received by programme and at an aggregate level, as well as broader performance information.

This is an area where there has been significant progress among the sample countries. In 2016, Kenya rolled out the Kenyan Single Registry (KSR), which is linked to the national registration database. It including information on beneficiaries of five social protection programmes including: the Old Age Grant, Disability Benefit, Orphans and Vulnerable Children's Cash Transfer, Hunger Safety Net programme, and World Food Programme's Cash for Assets scheme. Other countries might not be far behind: Zambia is currently in the process of designing and developing its Single Registry and information management system, to be hosted in the Ministry of Community Development, Mother and Child Health (World Bank, 2014).

Tanzania has constructed a Socio-Economic Database, which can potentially act as a bridge towards a single registry, but must improve the quality of its civil registration system in order to have accurate base-line records and population and welfare statistics. Tanzania also plans to consolidate a list of current beneficiaries of TASAF into a Unified Registry of Beneficiaries (UN Tanzania, n.d.). Mozambique is developing a management information system and plans to roll out a Single Registry as part of its National Development Strategy 2015-2035 (ILO, UNICEF and WFP, 2015).

Monitoring and evaluation are essential to improve social protection programmes and to establish social protection systems. Policy makers need up-to-date and reliable information on programmes' performance to ensure that their policy objectives are fulfilled and to better understand any potential weaknesses. Monitoring and evaluation are integral to the implementation of the social protection policy in Kenya, where a National Integrated Monitoring and Evaluation System (NIMES) includes specific indicators for social protection programmes. Overall however, such evidence remains sparse in sub-Saharan Africa, in particular in comparison with Latin America (Barrientos and Villa, 2013).

Notes

1. Annex 3.A1 provides an inventory and brief description of the major social assistance schemes in the six sample countries.

2. Annex 3.A2 describes the variation in different expenditure estimates by different agencies and proposes a "median" expenditure figure which is used for the calculations in this paragraph.

3. See, for example: Sudhanshu Handa et al. (2012), "Targeting effectiveness of Social Cash Transfer Programs in Three Africa Countries"; Slater R. and J. Farrington (2009), "Targeting of Social Transfers: A review for DFID", ODI Overseas Development Institute; Kakwani N. and H.H. Son (2006), "Evaluating Targeting Efficiency of Government Programmes: International Comparisons", *UN DESA Working Paper No. 13*.

4. Please see Williamson and Williams (2003), "The notional defined contribution model: an assessment of the strengths and limitations of a new approach to the provision of old age security" and "Parallel Lines: NDC Pensions and the Direction of Pension Reform" in Developed Countries Nonfinancial Defined Contribution Pension Schemes in a Changing Pension World. June 2012, 85-125 for a fuller description of the main issues around NDC arrangements.

5. For an assessment of their performance, please see Chłoń-Domińczak, A., D. Franco and E. Palmer (2012), "The First Wave of NDC Reforms: The Experiences of Italy, Latvia, Poland, and Sweden", in *Nonfinancial Defined Contribution Pension Schemes in a Changing Pension World*, pp. 31-84, World Bank, http://dx.doi.org/10.1596/9780821388488_CH02.

6. Poverty refers to USD 1.25 (PPP 2005) poverty line.

7. For a hypothetical impact analysis of eliminating subsidies and replacing them with a cash transfer scheme in Tanzania, see Younger, S. (2016), "The Impact Of Reforming Energy Subsidies, Cash Transfers, And Taxes On Inequality And Poverty In Ghana And Tanzania", *CEQ Working Paper*, No. 55, commitmentoequity.org/publications_files/Comparative/CEQ_WP55_Younger_Nov23_2016.pdf.

8. For more information, the World Bank publication *Reducing Old Age and Economic Vulnerabilities Why Uganda should Improve its Pension System* (2014) summarises the hypothetical cost of transitioning from an unfunded to a funded arrangement.

9. Not to be confused with a social registry. Please see Development Pathways (2016), "Single Registries and Social Registries: clarifying the terminological confusion", for an excellent explanation of the distinction, accessible here: developmentpathways.co.uk/resources/single-registries-social-registries-clarifying-terminological-confusion.

References

Alleyne, T. and M. Hussain (2013), "Energy Subsidy Reform in Sub-Saharan Africa: Experiences and Lessons", *African Departmental Paper* No. 13/2, International Monetary Fund, Washington, DC, imf.org/external/pubs/ft/dp/2013/afr1302.pdf.

Bahl, R.W., J. Martinez-Vazquez and J.M. Youngman (eds.) (2010), *Challenging the conventional wisdom on the property tax*, Lincoln Institute of Land Policy, Cambridge.

Barrientos, A. and J.M. Villa (2013), "Evaluating antipoverty transfer programmes in Latin America and sub-Saharan Africa: Better policies? Better politics?", *WIDER Working Paper* No. 2013/009, United Nations University, World Institute for Development Economics Research, wider.unu.edu/sites/default/files/WP2013-009.pdf.

Bastagli, F. et al. (2016), "Cash transfers: what does the evidence say? A rigorous review of impacts and the role of design and implementation features", Overseas Development Institute, London, odi.org/sites/odi.org.uk/files/resource-documents/11316.pdf.

Batte, E.R. (2016), "Government to insure farmers against risks", (Uganda) Daily Monitor, 27 July, monitor.co.ug/Magazines/Farming/Government-insure-farmers-risks/689860-3316896-15evahz/index.html.

Beegle, K. et al. (2016), *Poverty in a Rising Africa*, World Bank, Washington, DC, http://dx.doi.org/10.1596/978-1-4648-0723-7.

Blanchet, N. et al. (2012), "The Effect of Ghana's National Health Insurance Scheme on Health Care Utilisation", *Ghana Med J* 46(2), pp. 76–84.

Bloom, D. and J. Williamson (1997), "Demographic Transitions and Economic Miracles in Emerging Asia", National Bureau of Economic Research, *NBER Working Paper* No. 6268.

Bonilla Garcia, A. and J.V. Gruat (2003), "Social Protection, A life-cycle continuum investment for social justice, poverty reduction and sustainable development", Social Protection Sector, ILO, Geneva.

Bonner, C. and D. Spooner (2011), "Organizing in the Informal Economy: A Challenge for Trade Unions", *Internationale Politik und Gesellschaft*, ipg 2/2011, pp. 87-105.

Britto, P. et al. (2017), "Nurturing care: promoting early childhood development", *The Lancet* 389(10064), pp. 91–102, http://dx.doi.org/10.1016/S0140-6736(16)31390-3.

Brown, C., M. Ravallion and D. van de Walle (2016), "A Poor Means Test? Econometric Targeting in Africa", *NBER Working Paper* No. 22919, http://dx.doi.org/10.3386/w22919.

Budlender, D. and I. Woolard (2006), "The impact of the South African child support and old age grants on children's schooling and work", *TECL Paper* No. 36, International Labour Organization, Geneva.

Cabot Venton, C. et al. (2012), "The Economics of Early Response and Disaster Resilience: Lessons from Kenya and Ethiopia", *Economics of Resilience Final Report*, Department for International Development, London.

Carneiro, P. and J. Heckman (2003), "Human Capital Policy", *IZA Discussion Paper* No. 821.

Carranza, L., A. Melguizo and D. Tuesta (2012), "Matching Contributions in Colombia, Mexico, and Peru: Experiences and Prospects", in *Matching Contributions for Pensions: A Review of International Experience*, pp.193 – 213, World Bank, Washington, DC, http://dx.doi.org/10.1596/9780821394922_CH10.

Crivelli, E., R. De Mooij and M. Keen (2015), "Base Erosion, Profit Shifting and Developing Countries", *Working Paper* WP/15/118, Fiscal Affairs Department, International Monetary Fund, Washington, DC.

Coady, D. M. Grosh and J. Hoddinott (2004), *Targeting of Transfers in Developing Countries : Review of Lessons and Experience*, World Bank, Washington, DC, http://hdl.handle.net/10986/14902.

Cuevas, A. and I. Karpowicz (2016), "The Urgent Case for Pension Reform in Brazil", Diálogo a fondo blog, International Monetary Fund, Washington, DC, imf.org/external/np/blog/dialogo/120116.pdf.

Del Ninno, C., S. Coll-Black and P. Fallavier (2016), *Social Protection Programs for Africa's Drylands*, World Bank Studies, Washington, DC, http://dx.doi.org/10.1596/978-1-4648-0846-3.

Devereux, S. (2003), "Policy Options for Increasing the Contribution of Social Protection to Food Security", *ODI Forum for Food Security in Southern Africa Theme Paper*, Overseas Development Institute, odi.org/resources/docs/5607.pdf.

Devereux, S. (2002), "From Workfare to Fair Work: The Contribution of Public Works and Other Labour-Based Infrastructure Programmes to Poverty Alleviation", *Issues in Employment and Poverty Discussion Paper*, International Labour Organization, Geneva.

Dorfman, M.C. (2015), "Pension Patterns in Sub-Saharan Africa", *Social Protection and Labor Discussion Paper Series*, No. 1503, World Bank, Washington, DC, documents.worldbank.org/curated/en/743801468190183781/Pension-patterns-in-Sub-Saharan-Africa.

Durán-Valverde, F. et al. (2013), Innovations in extending social insurance coverage to independent workers: Experiences from Brazil, Cape Verde, Colombia, Costa Rica, Ecuador, Philippines, France and Uruguay, *Extension of Social Security (ESS) paper series*, No. 42, International Labour Office, Geneva.

Ethiopian News Agency (2016), "Small holder farmers to benefit from new agri-insurance", Addis Ababa, ena.gov.et/en/index.php/economy/item/924-small-holder-farmers-to-benefit-from-new-agri-insurance.

European Commission (2016), "The role of social partners in the design and implementation of policies and reforms", Employment, Social Affairs and Inclusion Department, European Commission, Brussels.

European Commission (2015), "Supporting Social Protection Systems", *Concept Paper* No. 4, Tools and Methods Series, Directorate General for International Cooperation and Development, European Commission, Brussels, ec.europa.eu/europeaid/sites/devco/files/supporting-social-protection-systems-20151125_en.pdf.

FAO (2015), "Empowering rural women through social protection", *Rural Transformations Technical Papers Series*, No. 2, Food and Agriculture Organisation of the United Nations, Rome, fao.org/3/a-i4696e.pdf.

Ferré, C. (2009), "Age at first child: Does education delay fertility timing? The case of Kenya," *World Bank Policy Research Working Papers*, Washington DC, http://dx.doi.org/10.1596/1813-9450-4833.

Fjeldstad, O.H., G. Chambas, and J.F. Brun (2014), "Local government taxation in Sub-Saharan Africa: A review and an agenda for research", *Working Paper* No. 2014-2, Chr. Michelsen Institute, Bergen.

Gentilini, U. (2015), "Entering the City: Emerging Evidence and Practices with Safety Nets in Urban Areas", *Discussion Paper* No. 1504, World Bank, Washington, DC.

Gertler, P. et al. (2014), "Labor market returns to an early childhood stimulation intervention in Jamaica", *Science* 344(6187), pp. 998-1001, http://dx.doi.org/10.1126/science.1251178.

Hallegatte, S. et al. (2017), *Unbreakable: Building the Resilience of the Poor in the Face of Natural Disasters*, World Bank, Washington, DC, openknowledge.worldbank.org/handle/10986/25335.

Handa, S. et al. (2015), "Impact of the Kenya Cash Transfer for Orphans and Vulnerable Children on early pregnancy and marriage of adolescent girls", *Soc Sci Med*, Vol. 141, pp. 36–45, http://dx.doi.org/10.1016/j.socscimed.2015.07.024.

Holmqvist, G. (2010), "Fertility impact of social transfers in Sub-Saharan Africa – What about pensions?", *BWPI Working Paper* 119, University of Manchester Brooks World Poverty Institute, ISBN 978-1-907247-18-7.

Humphreys, G. (2013), "Gabon gets everyone under one social health insurance roof," *Bulletin of the World Health Organization* 91, pp. 318-319, World Health Organization, Geneva.

ILO (2015), *Key Indicators of the Labour Market*, 9th edition (database), International Labour Organization, http://ilo.org/ilostat, (accessed June 2016).

ILO (2002), "Unprotected labour: What role for unions in the informal economy?" *Labour Education* 2002/2, No. 127, International Labour Organization, Geneva.

ILO, UNICEF, WFP (2015), "The Development of a Social Protection Floor in Mozambique", International Labour Organization, United Nations Children's Fund, United Nations World Food Programme, Maputo.

IMF (2016), *World Economic Outlook* (database), imf.org/en/data, (accessed April 2016).

IMF (2015), *How large are global energy subsidies?* (database), Fiscal Affairs Department, International Monetary Fund, accessed February 2017, imf.org/external/pubs/ft/survey/so/2015/NEW070215A.htm.

IMF (2011), "Resource mobilisation in developing countries", Fiscal Affairs Department, International Monetary Fund, Washington, DC.

IMF, OECD, UN and WBG (2016), "Enhancing the Effectiveness of External Support in Building Tax Capacity in Developing Countries", prepared for submission to G20 Finance Ministers by the International Monetary Fund, the OECD, the United Nations, and the World Bank Group, oecd.org/tax/enhancing-the-effectiveness-of-external-support-in-building-tax-capacity-in-developing-countries.pdf.

Jellema, J. et al. (2016) "The Impact of Taxes, Transfers, and Subsidies on Inequality and Poverty in Uganda," *CEQ Working Paper* No. 53, Commitment to Equity Institute, New Orleans.

Jones, R. (2010), "Health-care Reform in Korea", *Economics Department Working Papers* No. 797, OECD Publishing, Paris, http://dx.doi.org/10.1787/5kmbhk53x7nt-en.

Kidd, S., B. Gelders and D. Bailey-Athias (2017), "Exclusion by design: An assessment of the effectiveness of the proxy means test poverty targeting mechanism", *Extension of Social Security Working Papers Series*, No. 56, Development Pathways, International Labour Organization, Geneva.

Kopanyi, M. (2015), "Enhancing Own Revenues of Decentralised Entities in Rwanda Policy Challenges and Options in Reforming the Fixed-Asset Tax System", *Working Paper*, International Growth Centre, London.

Lagomarsino, G. et al. (2012), "Moving towards universal health coverage: health insurance reforms in nine developing countries in Africa and Asia", *The Lancet* 2012(380), pp. 933–943.

Lindebjerg, E.S, W. Peng and S. Yeboah (2015), "Do Policies for Phasing Out Fossil Fuel Subsidies Deliver What They Promise? Social Gains and Repercussions in Iran, Indonesia and Ghana", *UNRISD Working Paper* 2015-1, United Nations Research Institute for Social Development, Geneva.

Lustig, N. (2016), "Fiscal Policy, Inequality and the Poor in the Developing World", *Tulane Economics Working Paper Series*, No. 1612.

McCartney, M. and I. Roy (2016), "A Consensus Unravels: NREGA and the Paradox of Rules-Based Welfare in India", *European Journal of Development Research* 28(4), pp. 588 – 604, http://dx.doi.org/10.1057/ejdr.2015.32.

McCord, A. (2012), *Public Works and Social Protection in Sub-Saharan Africa. Do public works work for the poor?*, United Nations University Press.

Mulupi S., D. Kirigia and J. Chuma (2013), "Community perceptions of health insurance and their preferred design features: implications for the design of universal health coverage reforms in Kenya," *BMC Health Services Research*, 13, pp. 474–486.

OECD (2016a), *OECD Reviews of Health Systems: Mexico 2016*, OECD Publishing, Paris, http://dx.doi.org/10.1787/9789264230491-en.

OECD (2016b), *Making Cities Work for All: Data and Actions for Inclusive Growth*, OECD Publishing, Paris, http://dx.doi.org/10.1789/9789264263260-en.

OECD (2016c), *Climate Change Adaptation and Financial Protection: Synthesis of key findings from Colombia and Senegal*, unclassified document, OECD, Paris, oecd.org/officialdocuments/publicdisplaydocumentpdf/?cote=ENV/EPOC/WPCID(2016)4&docLanguage=En.

OECD (2015), "Base Erosion and Profit Shifting", OECD Publishing, Paris, oecd.org/g20/topics/taxation/beps.htm.

OECD (2012), "Social spending during the crisis: Social expenditure (SOCX) data update", OECD, Paris, oecd.org/els/social/expenditure.

OECD, CIAT and IDB (2016), *Taxing Wages in Latin America and the Caribbean*, OECD Publishing, Paris, http://dx.doi.org/10.1787/9789264262607-en.

Palermo, T. et al. (2016), "Unconditional government social cash transfer in Africa does not increase fertility", *J Popul Econ* 29(4), pp. 1083–1111, http://dx.doi.org/10.1007/s00148-016-0596-x.

Peralta-Alva, A. et al. (2017), "Macroeconomic Structural Policies and Income Inequality in Low-Income Developing Countries", *Staff Discussion Notes* No. 17/01, International Monetary Fund, Washington, DC.

Republic of Ethiopia (2016), *National Social Protection Strategy of Ethiopia*, Ministry of Labour and Social Affairs, Republic of Ethiopia, Addis Ababa, phe-ethiopia.org/resadmin/uploads/attachment-188-Ethiopia_National_Social_Protection.pdf.

Republic of Kenya (2011), *Kenya National Social Protection Policy*, Ministry of Gender, Children, and Social Development, Republic of Kenya, Nairobi.

Republic of Kenya and World Bank (2012), *Kenya Social Protection Sector Review*, World Bank, Ministry of State for Planning, Republic of Kenya, Nairobi, openknowledge.worldbank.org/handle/10986/16974.

Republic of South Africa (2017), "Budget Review", National Treasury, Republic of South Africa, Cape Town, treasury.gov.za/documents/national%20budget/2017/review/FullBR.pdf.

Republic of Uganda (2015), *National Social Protection Policy*, Ministry of Gender, Labour and Social Development, Republic of Uganda, Kampala.

Retirement Benefits Authority (2015), *Annual Report & Financial Statements 2015*, Retirement Benefits Authority, Republic of Kenya, Nairobi, rba.go.ke.

Schwarz, A.M. and M. Abels (2016), "Issues for Civil Service Pension Reform in Sub-Saharan Africa", *Social Protection and Labor Discussion Papers*, World Bank, Washington, DC, http://dx.doi.org/10.1596/25364.

Stewart, F. (2007), "Policy Issues for Developing Annuities Markets", *OECD Working Papers on Insurance and Private Pensions*, No. 2, OECD Publishing, Paris, http://dx.doi.org/10.1787/268701821137.

Suryahadi, Asep Yadi, Vita Febriany and Athia Yumna (2014), "Expanding social security in Indonesia: the processes and challenges", *UNRISD Working Paper* No. 2014-14.

UN DESA (2016), "Status of civil registration and vital statistics: African English-speaking countries", *CRVS Technical Report Series*, Vol. 3, United Nations Statistics Division, Demographic Statistics, Department of Economic and Social Affairs, New York.

UN DESA (2015), *World Population Prospects: The 2015 Revision*, United Nations Department of Economic and Social Affairs, New York.

UN Tanzania (n.d.), "Social Protection in Tanzania: Establishing a national system through consolidation, coordination and reform of existing measures", United Nations Tanzania, Dar es Salaam, unicef.org/tanzania/Fact_sheet.pdf.

UNICEF (2016), "Ethiopia - Social Protection: Access of the poor and vulnerable to basic social services. Good practices: Linking safety net clients with complementary social services", UNICEF Ethiopia, Addis Ababa.

van Klaveren, M., D. Gregory and T. Schulten (2015), *Minimum Wages, Collective Bargaining and Economic Development in Asia and Europe A Labour Perspective*, Palgrave MacMillan, London.

Varshney, D., D. Goel and J.V. Meenakshi (2014), "Impact of Mahatma Gandhi National Rural Employment Guarantee Act (MGNREGA) on Agriculture", *Working Paper*, isid.ac.in/~epu/acegd2014/papers/DeepakVarshney.pdf.

World Bank (2017), *World Development Indicators* (database), accessed April 2017, data.worldbank.org/products/wdi.

World Bank (2016a), *ASPIRE* (database), accessed June 2016, datatopics.worldbank.org/aspire.

World Bank (2016b), "Kenyan Farmers to Benefit from Innovative Insurance Program, press release", World Bank, Nairobi, worldbank.org/en/news/press-release/2016/03/12/kenyan-farmers-to-benefit-from-innovative-insurance-program.

World Bank (2015a), *Shockwaves: Managing the impact of climate change on poverty*, World Bank, Washington DC.

World Bank (2015b), *World Development Indicators* (database), accessed June 2015, http://data.worldbank.org/products/wdi.

World Bank (2015c), *Ethiopia Poverty Assessment 2014*, Report No. AUS6744, World Bank, Washington DC.

World Bank (2015d), *Statistical Capacity Indicator Dashboard* (database), datatopics.worldbank.org/statisticalcapacity/SCIdashboard.aspx.

World Bank (2014), *Zambia - Support for Development of an Integrated MIS and Single Registry of Beneficiaries Project*, Washington, DC, documents.worldbank.org/curated/en/595211468334888809/Zambia-Support-for-Development-of-an-Integrated-MIS-and-Single-Registry-of-Beneficiaries-Project.

World Bank (2008), *Africa's Future, Africa's Challenge, Early Childhood Care and Development in Sub-Saharan Africa*, (eds.) Marito Garcia, Alan Pence, Judith L. Evans, World Bank, Washington, DC.

World Bank (1993), *The East Asian Miracle: Economic Growth and Public Policy*, World Bank, Washington DC.

Younger, S. et al. (2016), "Fiscal incidence in Tanzania," *African Development Review* 28(3), pp. 264-276.

Annex 3.A1. Social assistance programmes and beneficiaries in the six countries

Ethiopia [Population: 99.5 million]
Pilot Social Cash Transfer Tigray: 3,767 households or 6,716 beneficiaries [2014]
Food Assistance under the Joint Emergency Operation: 2 500 000 [2013]
School feeding: 669 394 [2013]
Productive Safety Net Programme IV: 7 997 218 [2015]

Kenya [Population: 46.1 million]
Cash transfer for Orphans and Vulnerable Children; 1 265 000 [2015]
General Relief Food Distribution: 635 000 [2015]
Regular School Meals Programme: 791 000 [2015]
Food or Cash for Assets: 702 000 [2015]

Mozambique [Population 28.0 million]
Food Subsidy Programme: 291 604 [2013]
Direct Social Assistance: 125 000 [2013]
School Feeding: 427 000 [2011]
Social Productivity Programme: 10 000 [2014]
School fee waiver for secondary schools: 5 900 000 [2010]*

Tanzania [Population: 53.5 million]
Tanzanian Social Action Fund – Conditional Cash Transfer: 967 934 individuals [2014]
Most Vulnerable Children Programme: 570 000 [2010]
Food for Education: 1 275 000 [2011]
Food for Assets Creation: 58 202 [2010]
National Agricultural Input Voucher Scheme 1 800 000 [2012]

Uganda [Population 39.0 million]
Senior Citizens Grant: 113 000 [2014]
Protracted Relief and Recovery Operations: 352 495 [2013]
School Feeding Programme in Karamoja: 112 511 [2013]
Northern Uganda Social Action Fund II: 98 677 households involved in
income-generating activities [2016]
Inclusive Education for Girls Project: 1 182 [2013]

Zambia [Population: 16.2 million]
Social Cash Transfer Scheme: 171 000 [2015]
Orphans and Vulnerable Children: 204 251 [2013]
School Feeding Programme: 850 000 [2012]
C-SAFE Project: 22 412 [2012]

Description of social assistance programmes

Unconditional and conditional cash transfers and non-contributory social pensions

Ethiopia
<u>The Productive Safety Net Programme</u>
Targeted unconditional and conditional cash transfer

The combination of cash and food transfers is based on season and need, with food given primarily in the lean season between June and August. Vulnerable households receive six months of assistance annually to protect them from acute food insecurity. Additionally, food and cash assistance are extended by an additional three months under its Risk Financing Mechanism during periods when food insecure people are affected by unpredicted shocks. Able-bodied members of PSNP households must participate in productive activities that will build more resilient livelihoods, such as rehabilitating land and water resources and developing community infrastructure, including rural road rehabilitation and building schools and clinics.

Kenya

Cash transfers for Orphans and Vulnerable Children
Targeted unconditional cash transfer
The OVC programme provides cash transfers to eligible households. All supported households are subject to a proxy means test, are not allowed to receive funds from other programmes and must contain at least one orphan or vulnerable child under 18.

Older Persons Cash Transfer (OPCT)
The Older Persons Cash Transfer is a national programme that provides cash transfers to elderly persons. Although the 2010 Constitution defines the elderly as those aged 60 and over, the OPCT targets persons of age 65 or more who meet additional criteria, such as belonging to a poor and vulnerable household, non-enrolment in any other Cash Transfer programme, and other criteria. As of FY 2015/16, OPCT is estimated to cover 203 011 households, with a transfer amount of KES 2 000 per household per month delivered every two months.

Mozambique

Food subsidy programme
Targeted unconditional cash transfer
For people who are temporarily or permanently unable to work and unable to satisfy their subsistence needs. Eligibility is determined by proxy and direct means tests and health status.

Direct Social Support Programme
Targeted unconditional cash transfer
This programme addresses situations that require immediate intervention. It is for people in absolute poverty. Support is mainly through transfers in kind (food and clothing), aid for housing and payment of school fees.

Minimum Income for School Attendance
The programme provides a monthly cash transfer to poor households with children of school age.

Tanzania

Tanzanian Mainland Social Fund: Community-based Conditional Cash Transfer
Conditional cash transfer programmes provide grants to poor and vulnerable families, provided the families undertake specific actions, usually investments in human capital, such as keeping children at school or taking them to health centres on a regular basis.
TASAF uses a combination of four elements to identify beneficiaries:
- Selection of districts, wards and villages and allocation of resources to them
- Community identification of extremely poor and vulnerable households
- A proxy means test
- A community validation test to confirm the results of community identification and the proxy means test

Uganda
SAGE
Unconditional cash transfer
The Expanding Social Protection programme implements the Social Assistance Grants for Empowerment (SAGE) pilot scheme. which aims to generate evidence on the impact and feasibility of delivering small but regular and reliable direct income support to poor and vulnerable households and comprises a Senior Citizen Grant (SCG) for people aged 65 years and above and a vulnerability-targeted Vulnerable Family Grant.

Zambia
Public Welfare Assistance Scheme
Unconditional cash transfer
Offers social assistance to the most vulnerable to meet basic needs, which can include food, shelter, education, health and warm clothing. Communities help identify beneficiaries, prioritise needs and allocate resources. Beneficiaries usually include orphans and vulnerable children and households affected by HIV/AIDS.

Zambia Social Protection Expansion Programme
Unconditional cash transfer
This programme aims to improve the lives of the extremely poor and vulnerable by providing regular social cash transfers.

Public works, workfare and direct job creation

Ethiopia
The Productive Safety Net Programme

Kenya
Public works programmes
These are aimed at curbing Kenya's youth unemployment problem. They provide temporary employment and aim to increase youth employability through the development of labour intensive works, social services, and creation of private sector internships and training.

Mozambique
Social Development through Work programme
This is a transitional programme aimed at poor people able to work, integrating them in economic activity. The recipient works for eighteen months in a public or private institution and the programme contributes toward wages.

Food for work programme

This programme offers food for work in disaster stricken areas

Tanzania

Tanzanian Social Action Fund Public Works Programme

Targeting is based on:
- Poverty ranking noting in particular the illiteracy and children school dropout levels, the percentage of poor female headed households and the lack of job opportunities.
- Shocks like seasonal droughts and crop failures (food shortages) and other disasters.

- Intra-District/Island criteria focusing on communities that are: (a) Inaccessible by existing infrastructure (b) Located in remote areas (c) Persistently short of food. (d) Lack access to cash income.

Uganda

There are a number of programmes with public works components concentrated in northern Uganda. These programmes include the Northern Uganda Social Action Fund, the Karamoja Livelihoods Improvement Programme and the Agricultural Livelihoods Recovery Programme. The objectives of the public works programmes include the creation of community assets, the provision of food items to households affected by famine and the transfer of cash transfer to poor households with labour capacity.

Zambia

<u>Work for food programme</u>

This has operated in various areas, including peri-urban areas, and it aims to promote the development of the poor through participatory and community based public works. Beneficiaries are the extreme poor but able-bodied whose family members had lost jobs, or were victims of natural disasters, or were women and orphans.

Other forms of social assistance
All countries
School feeding schemes

Ethiopia
Health Sector Development Programme
Health services are provided free or at a subsidised cost to the poor. A study conducted in 2009/10 based on 2007/08 data found that out-of-pocket payments constitute 37% of the total health expenditure.

Kenya
Health
The private sector share of total health expenditure decreased from a high of 54% in 2001/02 (of which 44.8% constituted out of pocket expenditure) to 37% in 2009/10 (of which 24% constituted OOP expenditure). This decrease in OOP was primarily driven by increases in government and donor resources.

Mozambique
Public health expenditure
The health system is composed of public/private for profit and non-profit private sector, the public sector being the main provider however with a network covering only about 60% of the population.
Targeted subsidy
Bread

Tanzania
Targeted subsidies
National Agricultural Input Voucher Scheme (NAIVS)

Zambia
Targeted subsidies
Maize

Annex 3.A2. Variation in different expenditure estimates of social protection programmes

The publicly available information on the subject creates a confusing record. Table 3.A2.1 presents data on public social protection excluding health benefits in kind as a percentage of GDP from the ILO's Social Protection database and in the case of Kenya, a later observation reported in the ILO's World Social Protection Report 2014/15. There are implausibly large year to year fluctuations even within a particular source (for instance, the IMF Government Finance Statistics, or the ILO Social Security Data Base) in Ethiopia, Kenya and Mozambique.

Table 3.A2.1. Public social protection expenditure excluding health benefits in kind, as a percentage of GDP

Country	Year	% of GDP	Source of information
Ethiopia	2005	2.1	International Monetary Fund (Government Finances Statistics)
Ethiopia	2008	0.5	ILO Social Security Inquiry database
Ethiopia	2010	0.6	International Monetary Fund (Government Finances Statistics)
Kenya	2005	1.0	International Monetary Fund (Government Finances Statistics)
Kenya	2008	1.7	International Monetary Fund (Government Finances Statistics)
Kenya	2009	1.9	International Monetary Fund (Government Finances Statistics)
Kenya	2010	1.3	International Monetary Fund (Government Finances Statistics)
Kenya	2011	1.0	International Monetary Fund (Government Finances Statistics)
Kenya	2013	0.9	World Social Protection Report 2014/15
Mozambique	2005	0.4	ILO Social Security Inquiry database
Mozambique	2007	0.8	Government
Mozambique	2010	2.0	ILO Social Security Inquiry database
Tanzania	2005	1.4	ILO Social Security Inquiry database
Tanzania	2007	1.8	ILO Social Security Inquiry database
Tanzania	2008	1.8	ILO Social Security Inquiry database
Tanzania	2010	2.3	ILO Social Security Inquiry database
Uganda	2005	1.2	International Monetary Fund (Government Finances Statistics)
Uganda	2007	0.9	International Monetary Fund (Government Finances Statistics)
Uganda	2008	1.1	International Monetary Fund (Government Finances Statistics)
Uganda	2010	1.5	International Monetary Fund (Government Finances Statistics)
Uganda	2011	1.2	International Monetary Fund (Government Finances Statistics)
Zambia	2007	1.7	ILO Social Security Inquiry database
Zambia	2010	1.8	ILO Social Security Inquiry database
Zambia	2011	1.8	ILO Social Security Inquiry database

The situation becomes even more confused when data from the World Bank's State of Social Safety Nets Report 2015 is added into the mix (Table 3.A2.2).

The situation undoubtedly arises from poor data on the functional classification of government expenditure in the six countries and variable methods for imputation even within some of the same sources at different points in time. There is no published informational basis on which the discrepancies can be accounted for.

Table 3.A2.2. **Social safety net expenditure**
Per cent of GDP

Country	Year	% of GDP
Ethiopia	2013	1.1
Kenya	2014	2.7
Mozambique	2010	1.3
Tanzania	2009	0.3
Uganda	2014	1.0
Zambia	2011	0.5

Source: Honorati, M., U. Gentilini, and R.G. Yemtsov (2015), State of Social Safety Nets 2015, World Bank, Washington, DC, documents.worldbank.org/curated/en/415491467994645020/The-state-of-social-safety-nets-2015.

This creates a major problem in determining the degree of social assistance effort in each country. The following decisions were made:

Ethiopia	The World Bank estimate of 1.1%
Kenya	The mean of all the observations: 1.5%
Mozambique	The World Bank estimate of 1.3%
Tanzania	The mean of all the observations: 1.5%
Uganda	The mean of all the observations: 1.1%
Zambia	The mid-point between the World Bank estimate and the most recent ILO estimate: 1.2%

ORGANISATION FOR ECONOMIC CO-OPERATION AND DEVELOPMENT

The OECD is a unique forum where governments work together to address the economic, social and environmental challenges of globalisation. The OECD is also at the forefront of efforts to understand and to help governments respond to new developments and concerns, such as corporate governance, the information economy and the challenges of an ageing population. The Organisation provides a setting where governments can compare policy experiences, seek answers to common problems, identify good practice and work to co-ordinate domestic and international policies.

The OECD member countries are: Australia, Austria, Belgium, Canada, Chile, the Czech Republic, Denmark, Estonia, Finland, France, Germany, Greece, Hungary, Iceland, Ireland, Israel, Italy, Japan, Korea, Latvia, Luxembourg, Mexico, the Netherlands, New Zealand, Norway, Poland, Portugal, the Slovak Republic, Slovenia, Spain, Sweden, Switzerland, Turkey, the United Kingdom and the United States. The European Union takes part in the work of the OECD.

OECD Publishing disseminates widely the results of the Organisation's statistics gathering and research on economic, social and environmental issues, as well as the conventions, guidelines and standards agreed by its members.

OECD DEVELOPMENT CENTRE

The OECD Development Centre was established in 1962 as an independent platform for knowledge sharing and policy dialogue between OECD member countries and developing economies, allowing these countries to interact on an equal footing. Today, 27 OECD countries and 25 non-OECD countries are members of the Centre. The Centre draws attention to emerging systemic issues likely to have an impact on global development and more specific development challenges faced by today's developing and emerging economies. It uses evidence-based analysis and strategic partnerships to help countries formulate innovative policy solutions to the global challenges of development.

For more information on the Centre and its members, please see *www.oecd.org/dev*.

OECD PUBLISHING, 2, rue André-Pascal, 75775 PARIS CEDEX 16
(41 2016 19 1 P) ISBN 978-92-64-27421-1 – 2017